HISTORY OF THE ROYAL NAVY

ROBERT JACKSON

p

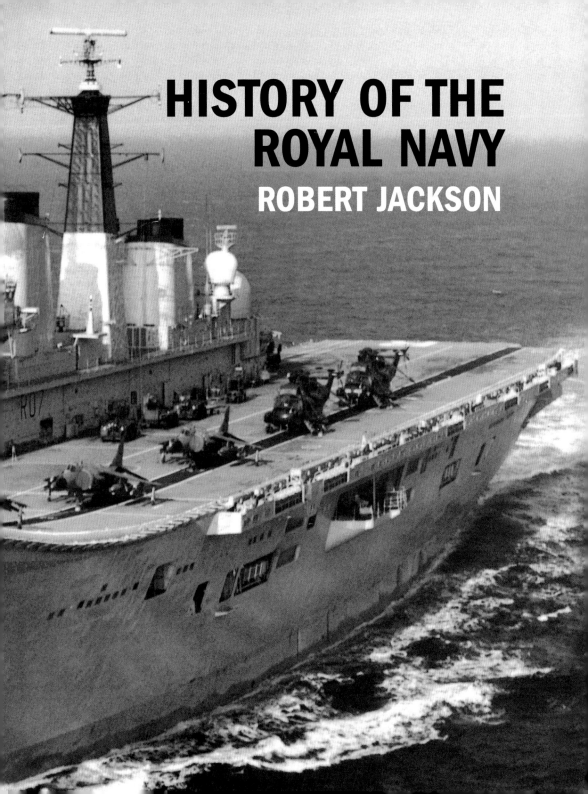

HISTORY OF THE
ROYAL NAVY

ROBERT JACKSON

This is a Parragon Book
This edition published in 2002
Parragon
Queen Street House
4 Queen Street
Bath BA1 1HE, UK

ISBN 0-75257-988-6

Editorial and design by
Amber Books Ltd
Bradley's Close
74-77 White Lion Street
London N1 9PF

Design: Jeremy Williams

Printed in Spain

Picture Acknowledgments
All pictures TRH Pictures except the following:
Hugh Cowin: 94 (top)
Robert Hunt Library: 66
Robert Jackson: 32, 62, 70, 72, 77, 86-87, 90, 91,
94 (bottom), 95 (both

Artwork Acknowledgements
All artworks Istituto Geografico De Agostini

Previous pages: HMS *Ocean* undergoing sea trials.

CONTENTS

Somes of yron Gounepowder

CHAPTER 1

THE AGE OF SAIL

Between the Battle of the Spanish Armada and the Napoleonic Wars, the Royal Navy underwent a tremendous transformation. Other nations might match them in calibre of guns and quality of building, but it was superior British tactics and discipline that won time and time again.

'AD896. The same year, the forces in East Anglia and Northumbria greatly harassed Wessex along the south coast with raiding bands, most of all with the ash-ships they had built many years before. Then King Alfred commanded longships to be built against the ash-ships. They were nearly twice as long as the others; some had sixty oars, some more. They were both swifter and steadier, also higher than the

ABOVE: This engraving well illustrates the close range at which naval battles were fought during the age of sail. They were slogging matches, the aim being to dismast an opponent.

LEFT: Henry VIII's Grace à Dieu was huge for her day. Her main innovation was the introduction of the heavy gun, mounted on the lower deck and fired through ports in the ship's side.

others; nor were they in the Frisian manner or the Danish, but as he himself thought might be most useful.'

In those few lines, the Anglo-Saxon Chronicles record the beginnings of English sea power. Although every monarch who succeeded Alfred of Wessex throughout mediaeval times had fighting ships of some sort at his disposal, it was to be more than 500 years before a regular English fleet – a 'Navy Royal' – came into being.

Its architect was Henry VIII, and his naval planning was spurred by the activities of James IV of Scotland, who already had several powerful warships at his disposal when Henry succeeded to the throne in 1509. From his father, Henry inherited a small fleet headed by two large carracks (ocean-going merchantmen distinguished by a high super-structure fore and aft) called the *Regent* and the *Sovereign*.

Henry ordered the latter to be rebuilt and provided with a strengthened hull, presumably to carry new and heavier guns.

Over the next few years other large ships were built, the foremost of which were the *Mary Rose*, *Peter Pomegranate* and *Henry Grace-à-Dieu*. The latter, also known as the *Great Harry*, was the mightiest warship afloat. Displacing 1,016 tonnes (1,000 tons) she was commissioned as a replacement for the *Regent*, lost in action in 1512, and was launched in 1514. Other large vessels added to Henry's growing fleet were the *Gabriel Royal*, *Katherine Fortileza*, *Maria de Loreto*, *John Baptist*, *Great Nicholas*, *Christ*, *Mary James*, *Mary George*, *Great Elizabeth* and *Spaniard*, all converted merchantmen and some built in foreign shipyards.

One thing that Henry VIII did inherit from his father was a sound base of naval gunnery. From the start of his reign, Henry VII had employed French and Spanish gun-founders, and by 1496 they were producing wrought iron guns and iron shot. The first attempt to cast iron guns in England was made in 1508, and by 1510 breech-loaders with separate chambers were being successfully cast. A year later, Henry VIII established a foundry at Hounsditch, London, one of its principal tasks being to produce guns to arm his fleet.

The first ship known to have been designed to carry guns on a gun deck above the orlop (the lowest deck of a ship with three or more decks) was the *Mary Rose*, and the idea of firing guns through ports cut in the side of the ship was developed sometime between 1505 and 1509. The *Mary Rose* almost certainly had lidded gun ports from the beginning, and so marked a revolution in warship design.

In 1512, England joined Spain in an alliance against France, which was intent on conquering Italy, and Henry was able to muster a fleet of 25 warships to attack French shipping and harbours and to land troops on French soil. In August, the English engaged a combined Franco-Breton fleet of 22 ships at Brest (it was during this engagement that the *Regent* was

Also Known as the 'Great Harry', the Henri Grace-à-Dieu *was commissioned to replace the* Regent, *lost in action in 1512. Launched in 1514, she was the mightiest warship afloat at 1016 tonnes (1000 tons) and together with the* Mary Rose *and* Peter Pomegranate, *formed the core of Henry VIII's naval reconstruction program in the first quarter of the century.*

lost). After a heavy exchange of gun-fire she grappled with the Breton warship *Cordelière*; the latter caught fire and exploded, destroying both vessels with heavy loss of life.

Despite this loss, the English fleet under Henry's Lord Admiral, Sir Edward Howard, retained command of the English Channel. The fleet was now divided into three squadrons – Westward, Northward and Dover and Calais – and provision was made to keep the ships victualled and the sailors paid during the winter of 1512–23.

By the spring of 1513 – about the time that the *Henry Grace-à-Dieu* was launched – Sir Edward Howard had 23 'Royal' fighting ships at his disposal, in addition to 27 others, some hired from the Spaniards, supported by a considerable fleet of supply vessels. In April, Howard launched another attack on Brest, but this time he encountered a force of heavily armed enemy galleys under the leadership of a skilled and experienced sea fighter, Pregent de Bidoux, who sank one of his ships and badly damaged another. Howard boarded Bidoux's vessel, but was cut off and killed when the English fleet scattered in confusion, possibly under fire from shore batteries.

During the remainder of 1513, Henry's fleet was occupied in supporting an English invasion of France, which began in June when 10,000 troops were landed at Calais. James IV of Scotland seized the opportunity to declare war on England and allied his fleet with France's, but the Scots' war effort was shattered by their defeat at Flodden in September, and the death of James.

MARY ROSE

Henry continued to fight the French, even though his Spanish allies had signed a separate peace treaty with them, and in April 1514 a fleet of 45 ships – his own and hired merchantmen, led by the *Henry Grace-à-Dieu* – ferried another 8000 men across the Channel to reinforce the Calais garrison. In June, however, possibly as a result of intervention by a new Pope, Leo X, Henry decided to call a truce.

At the end of hostilities Henry had a fleet of 30 ships, nine of which had been built since 1512. Significantly, the navy was now operating independently of the army, and was supported by new dockyards and storehouses. For the first time, an efficient naval logistics system was in place, and the fleet was maintained in fighting trim, the larger ships being repaired and renovated.

In October 1515, another formidable fighting ship joined the fleet. Known officially as the *Princess Mary*, or sometimes

*ABOVE: The **Ark Royal** was Lord Howard of Effingham's flagship during the Battle of the Spanish Armada. She was originally commissioned for Sir Walter Raleigh's colonial adventures.*

the *Mary Imperial*, she was popularly called the *Great Galley*, and according to contemporary accounts she carried over 200 guns, 70 of which were brass. Fourteen of these were mounted, seven on each side, on a gun deck above the oarsmen. Main propulsion was provided by 120 oars, but she also had four masts. She remained in service as a galleasse (the term for a hybrid oared warship with sails) until 1536, when she was rebuilt as a pure sailing ship and renamed the *Great Bark*.

A further outbreak of hostilities with France in 1522–25 saw renewed cross-Channel raiding by Henry's warships. For the next few years, Henry was more preoccupied with his notoriously complicated private life and with war against Scotland than with maritime affairs, but in 1545 full-scale war with France again erupted, and in July of that year, French warships made a massive incursion into the Solent almost unopposed, the main body of the English fleet being confined to Portsmouth because of adverse winds. During this incident (on 19 July), the *Mary Rose* – which had been rebuilt in 1536 – foundered and sank with the loss of her captain, Sir George Carew, and about 500 soldiers and seamen. The French claimed to have sunk her, which was not true; the real reason was overloading, which had brought her gun deck too close to the waterline. A strong gust of wind caused her to heel over and water gushed in through her gun ports, which were open ready for action.

The French commander, Claude d'Annebaut, abandoned his plans to attack Portsmouth and sailed to Boulogne, where

he put ashore some 7000 troops. Early in August, a gale drove his ships back across the Channel, where they were engaged by the English fleet under Lord Lisle. There was a desultory exchange of gunfire that lasted until dark, when both sides withdrew. On 2 September, Lisle attacked Le Treport, taking and burning the town along with 30 ships in the harbour.

Henry VIII died on 28 January 1547, six months after peace was finally concluded with France. He left behind him a fleet in existence, and the means to sustain it, but it had no regular body of officers and men. There was a nucleus of so-called 'standing officers' – gunners, boatswains and carpenters – who maintained the ships when they were laid up, and they would be joined by the ship's master, sailing master, cook and purser as individual ships were about to be commissioned. The seamen themselves were recruited as the occasion demanded; many, but by no means all, were recruited forcibly.

A STERN TEST

It was during the reign of Henry's daughter, Elizabeth I, that England's navy faced its sternest test. In the 1580s, Philip II of Spain, no admirer of the Protestant Elizabeth I of England, launched what the Spaniards called the 'Enterprise of England'. First, the English fleet would be destroyed, and then a large expeditionary force, brought partly from Spain by the ships of the Spanish Armada (the name means simply 'Fleet') and partly from the Spanish-controlled Netherlands, would be landed on the shores of England to smash the English armies and restore England to Catholicism under Philip's careful guidance. The target date for the invasion was August 1587.

Elizabeth already knew about the invasion plans, and authorised the expansion of her navy. Eleven new ships were completed in 1586 and two more in 1587; they included the *Vanguard*, the *Rainbow* and the *Ark Royal*, each over 406 tonnes (400 tons). She also instructed her 'gentleman adventurer', Sir Francis Drake – already notorious for his

LEFT: Martin Frobisher was one of Queen Elizabeth I's most accomplished seamen. He harboured a deep dislike of Sir Francis Drake, of whom he was fiercely jealous.

piratical activities against Spanish merchant shipping – to launch what amounted to a pre-emptive attack on the Spanish fleet. Assembling a force of 23 ships, Drake accordingly attacked the Spanish harbour of Cadiz on 19 April 1587, destroying or capturing 24 Spanish vessels, some of them large and powerful, together with large quantities of stores and equipment. For several months, Spanish warships scoured the ocean for Drake's elusive squadron; the Spaniards returned home, their ships weather-beaten, their supplies exhausted and their crews stricken by disease, in October 1587, by which time Drake had long since been back in England.

This action, and other factors, delayed the sailing of the Armada for the best part of a year, and had it not been for the energy and efficiency of its commander, the Duke of Medina Sidonia, it would probably never have sailed at all. The Duke eventually had 130 ships at his disposal, but only about 30 were properly armed warships, and only six in the entire fleet carried more than 40 guns, which at that time was the normal level for any English ship of more than 254 tonnes (250 tons). Moreover, many of the guns were old, were not designed for use on board ship, and were manned by soldiers with no experience of sea warfare.

The English, meanwhile, had been mobilizing their fleet since the beginning of 1588, having realised that Drake's attack on Cadiz had merely postponed the planned invasion. All the maritime resources of the nation were mustered, and by midsummer 1588 the Lord Admiral, Lord Howard of Effingham, had 197 ships at his disposal. Of these, 34 were the Queen's own ships; a further 53 smaller vessels were 'taken up' for service and paid for by the Queen; and another 23, financed in a similar manner, were under the command of Lord Henry Seymour. The rest of the fleet was provided by private contribution; for example, 30 were provided and paid for by the City of London, and 34 more – commanded by Sir Francis Drake – were furnished by individual nobles and wealthy merchants.

During the early months of 1588, the ships of the fleet were scattered at locations all around the English coastline, and on Drake's advice, Lord Howard issued orders for them to concentrate on Plymouth. The assembly took some time, and it was fortunate for the English that the Armada had suffered further misfortune, having been scattered by a south-westerly gale a couple of weeks after it left Lisbon, on 18 May. Adverse winds also frustrated an attempt by Howard to attack the Armada at Coruna, where its ships had sought shelter. The English fleet returned to Plymouth on 12 July, its provisions exhausted and many of its ships in need of repair. It was still there when the Spaniards were sighted off the Lizard. Hurriedly completing their revictualling, the English captains managed to sail out of Plymouth Sound against the adverse wind, and on 20 July, in thick, drizzly weather, the two fleets made contact.

SERIOUS LOSSES

At this point the Armada was sailing in a formation that had the main fighting strength and the troopships in the centre and two wings trailing to form the characteristic crescent shape of a galley fleet in battle order. To open the battle, Lord Howard sent his pinnace, the *Disdain*, forward to fire a single shot by way of a challenge; then he led his squadron to attack the seaward wing of the Armada, while Drake's squadron attacked the other. Sweeping round the two wings, where the best Spanish fighting ships were positioned, they raked them with continuous fire, and although it did not do a great deal of damage, the Spaniards suffered two serious losses during this early phase of the action. Firstly, the *Nuestra Senora del Rosario* lost her bowsprit and foremast in a collision, and then the *San Salvador* was badly damaged by a powder explosion.

That night, Howard ordered the English fleet to follow the stern lantern of Drake's *Revenge*, but during the night the lantern suddenly went out and when morning came the fleet

*BELOW: **Warships of Cromwell's navy: the Assurance, Elizabeth and Tiger. Another two-decker, not in this engraving, was the Fairfax, named after Cromwell's trusted lieutenant, Sir Thomas Fairfax.***

was badly dispersed. Drake later claimed that he had gone off to investigate some ships he had sighted, and that it was mere coincidence that he had come alongside the crippled *Rosario*, accepted her captain's surrender, and claimed her as his prize – a very wealthy one, as it turned out, as she carried a pay chest containing 50,000 gold ducats. Drake's action aroused the furious jealousy of some of his colleagues. Later, the English also took possession of the abandoned wreck of the *San Salvador*.

For the next three days, Wednesday to Friday, the two fleets moved slowly up the Channel before very light breezes. Saturday morning found them off the Isle of Wight, where there was more heavy fighting. The threat of a possible landing on the Solent was averted by an attack on the seaward wing of the Spanish fleet, forcing it to alter course out to sea, but the crisis of the battle was still to come. The Armada, still intact and undefeated, was now approaching the Netherlands, where the Spanish army under the Duke of Parma was waiting for it. Medina Sidonia now chose to abandon his original orders, which were to embark Parma's army from Flanders – an operation that would have been impossible in any case, as the Spaniards lacked the flat-bottomed craft necessary to cross the shallow waters of the Flanders Banks. Instead, the Spanish admiral anchored off Calais, where he received the unwelcome news that Parma's

army would not be ready to embark for another week. This left Medina Sidonia in a dangerous position, with his ships in an exposed anchorage and around 140 English vessels anchored close to windward. Nevertheless, Parma was only 30 miles away at Dunkirk, and the English commanders, unaware of the delay, believed that his army might arrive at any moment. At all costs, the Armada had to be broken, and quickly.

HEAVY GUNS

On the night of Sunday 28 July, the English launched eight small fireships at the Spaniards. Two were grappled and towed aside, but the rest menaced the Spanish ships, which cut or slipped their cables and put out to sea. Only Medina Sidonia's flagship and four other vessels retained a semblance of cohesion during the manoeuvre; the rest were scattered, their formation broken.

Howard's ships, upwind and to seaward, now closed in on the Spaniards like terriers, approaching to 'within half a musket shot' – about 45m (150ft) – to pound the enemy with their heavy guns. For nine hours the battle went on, until the English ships ran out of powder and shot. One Spanish ship, the *Maria Juan*, was sunk; two more were driven onto the shoals and taken by the Dutch; and many others were damaged. The damage to the English ships was negligible.

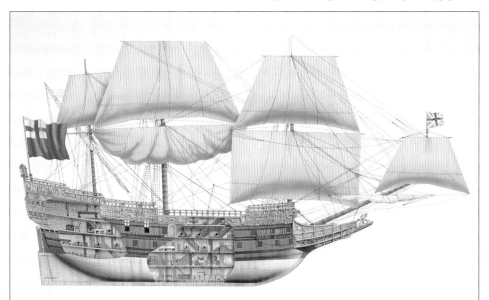

*The **Sovereign** of the Seas was commissioned by King Charles I in 1637. She was the biggest fighting vessel ever constructed in England up to that time. She was to serve the nation well for many years to come.*

*ABOVE: **Engagement between the British and Dutch fleets off the North Foreland, 28 September 1652. The interests of Britain and Holland clashed continually during this period.***

It says much for the courage and discipline of the Spaniards that they succeeded in restoring a fighting formation. But the weather was now worsening, and the Armada was being driven inexorably towards the Zealand Banks. Then, early on Tuesday 30 July, the wind suddenly backed, enabling the fleet to put out into the North Sea. The English continued to follow it, despite their lack of ammunition, speculating as to which friendly port the Spaniards might be making for.

Indeed, Medina Sidonia might easily have decided to head for Hamburg, Denmark, Norway or Scotland. Instead, he opted for the long and dangerous route home around the north of Scotland. On 2 August, past the latitude of the Firth of Forth, the English at last abandoned their pursuit of the battered Armada, which struggled on to face the autumn gales of the North Atlantic. Sixty-seven ships reached Spain, with many men dead or dying. Some captains, despite dire warnings, took a gamble and sought refuge on the shores of Ireland, where almost all were drowned or slaughtered and their ships destroyed. At least a third of the Armada's complement of 29,000 seamen and soldiers never returned home. It was a catastrophe that plunged the whole of Spain into mourning, and it turned the tide of Spanish expansion.

During the reign of James I – James IV of Scotland, who succeeded Elizabeth on her death in 1603 – the English fleet fell into sorry neglect. Even so, British merchant adventurers continued to further Britain's presence on the ocean; with the union of the crowns of England and Scotland, maritime trade was now a matter of joint enterprise. Nevertheless, James did commission one new warship. She was the *Prince Royal*, and her builder was Phineas Pett. She was not a great success; the longest voyage she made was to Spain, and after only 10 years, she had to be rebuilt at three-quarters of her original cost. Although the *Prince Royal*'s design faults brought much scorn down on Pett, in 1637 King Charles I commissioned his son, Peter, to build a very large warship of 1663 tonnes (1637 tons). Named *Sovereign of the Seas*, she was the biggest fighting vessel ever built in England up to that time, and she carried over 100 guns mounted in three tiers, making her the first three-decker man-of-war. She was lavishly decked out with ornate carvings and other trappings. Later, her gun decks were reduced to two. She served the nation well for many years; in Cromwell's day, the 'Royal' was dropped from her name, but after the Restoration, she became the *Royal Sovereign* and was still a flagship at the Battle of Barfleur against the French in 1692. Five years later she caught fire in the Medway and was destroyed, the consequence of a lighted candle left untended by a careless cook. She was 60 years old.

It was during the reign of Charles I, when the British Navy was mainly involved in hunting down pirates, that the Dutch began to present a serious challenge to Britain's sea trade. It was a curious state of affairs, for although the commercial interests of the two nations clashed everywhere, they were united against their old enemy, Spain, particularly in the West Indies, where both the Dutch and English had begun to settle.

The rivalry erupted into open warfare in 1652, soon after the end of the English Civil War. It began with a confrontation between the English 'Soldier-Admiral' Robert Blake and the Dutch Admiral Marten Tromp off Dover (the Dutchman – so it is claimed – had refused to lower his topsails in salute), and ended in July 1653, after a series of engagements that produced no decisive victories, in the Battle of Scheviningen, when Tromp was killed.

At the close of this first naval war with the Dutch, the British fleet comprised some 160 vessels of all types, and the

*BELOW: **The second Battle of Schooneveld was fought between the British and Dutch fleets on 4 June 1673. The Dutch seamen were every bit as skilled and capable as their opponents.***

disciplined rule of Oliver Cromwell had gone a long way towards eliminating the inefficiency and corruption that had existed in Charles I's time. The navy was now governed by commissioners, appointed by Parliament, and led by senior army officers: the 'Generals-at-sea', of which Robert Blake was one. Another was George Monck, made Duke of Albermarle by Charles II, who was greeted by Monck when he landed at Dover from exile in May 1660.

SEA BATTLES

By 1665, the British and Dutch (the latter now allied with France) were at war again, and during the months that followed some of the fiercest sea battles ever fought occurred in the 100 miles of North Sea that lay between the two countries. Apart from a brief period when the British fleet was led by the Duke of York, later James II, who won an early victory off Lowestoft and destroyed the Dutch flagship, joint command was exercised by Monck and by Prince Rupert, who had fought ably at sea as well as on land during the English Civil War.

At the end of May 1666 the British received a report, which turned out to be false, that the French fleet had sailed to join the Dutch. Prince Rupert took half the British fleet to intercept it. Monck was left to face a greatly superior Dutch fleet – 44 ships against 80 – under the command of the brilliant Admiral de Ruyter. Battle was joined on 1 June 1666,

and at the end of the second day the British faced even greater odds when de Ruyter was reinforced by 16 more ships. Monck detached his most damaged ships and sent them home, protecting them in a fighting retreat that lasted throughout the third day. It was successful, although there was one major casualty. The veteran three-decker *Royal Prince* ran aground on the Galloper Shoal, 20 miles off the coast of East Anglia, and was surrounded. She was set on fire by the Dutch, who took her whole company prisoner, including her captain, Sir George Ayscue.

That evening, another fleet was sighted, approaching from the English Channel. It turned out to be Prince Rupert's force, and its timely arrival enabled the British to attack with renewed vigour on the fourth day of battle, until a thick summer fog descended and brought an end to the engagement. The 'Four Days Battle' had been costly for the British, who had lost 17 ships – eight sunk or burnt and nine captured – together with 5000 men killed and another 3000 taken prisoner.

Two months later, on 25 July 1666, after both fleets had returned home to lick their wounds and make repairs, they met again off the North Foreland, the easternmost point of Kent. On this occasion the British got the upper hand and chased de Ruyter back to Holland, sinking two of his ships and then attacking 12 merchantmen in harbour. They destroyed no fewer than 150 vessels, as well as burning and pillaging villages and storehouses.

In 1667, following the ravages of the plague and the disastrous Great Fire of London, King Charles, desperately short of money, decided to lay up his fleet in the River Medway. It was a fatal error. In June, de Ruyter blockaded the mouth of the Thames and Medway, and sailed boldly into the latter, breaking the defensive chain that was stretched across it. He bombarded the forts, destroyed many of the ships anchored off Chatham, and sailed home with several prizes – including the *Royal Charles*, the fleet flagship. It was the most daring and skilful sea raid launched on the British Isles since the days of the Vikings, and it was nothing short of a national humiliation.

A CAREER AT SEA

The wars with Holland, fought against an enemy every bit as skilled as the British in naval tactics and seamanship, forced the rapid development of British naval power. The merchant and war fleets were now separate entities, and the navy was armed with ships built from the outset as fighting vessels. Tactics were evolved whereby ships fought in squadrons, rather than as individual units. Specialized signals were devised, using flags to indicate a commander's intentions and

ABOVE: A sea battle of the American War of Independence: the American Bon Homme Richard *engaging the British frigate* Scrapis. *Such battles starved British troops of essential supplies.*

to issue orders. Young men from the leading families of the land began to look to the sea as a career, entering the Naval Service, the King's Service, as boys. And from about 1670, that Service came to be known as the Royal Navy.

King Charles II died in 1685 and was succeeded by his brother, the Duke of York, who was enthroned as King James II. His reign was short-lived and he was succeeded by William, Prince of Orange-Nassau, who became King William III. The accession of this Protestant monarch signalled a renewal of hostilities with England's old enemy, Catholic France, whose king, Louis XIV, had given refuge to the exiled James II.

The struggle was to last for more than a century, and it began with one of the most decisive victories in British naval history. On 19 May 1692, an Anglo-Dutch fleet of 99 ships engaged 44 French vessels off Barfleur. In a battle lasting four days, three French ships, including the French flagship, were driven ashore near Cherbourg and set on fire, while 12 more – all three-deckers – were destroyed in La Hogue Bay, on the eastern side of the Cherbourg peninsula. The War of the Spanish Succession of 1702–13 (which arose from the fact that the King of Spain had died childless and bequeathed his dominions to Philip of Anjou, raising the spectre of a Franco-Spanish Alliance), saw the Royal Navy's activities spread to the Mediterranean, where Gibraltar was captured by a force of Royal Marines in 1704. Other eighteenth-century wars took the Royal Navy's squadrons to the Caribbean, Canada and India, and on an expedition around the world. But while the Royal Navy's operations continued to evolve worldwide, the ships that conducted them remained virtually

*ABOVE: **Admiral Lord Hood was First Sea Lord at the beginning of the long war with revolutionary France in 1793. He was fortunate to have excellent subordinates – including Nelson.***

unchanged. Only the first-raters of 100 guns could match Charles I's *Sovereign of the Seas* for size, and for most of the century there were only six or seven of them. The rest were mostly fifth-raters up to third-raters of 30–80 guns, displacing 609–1372 tonnes (600–1350 tons), with gundecks 38–48m (125–160ft) in length.

But there was one innovation that was to play a key part in naval operations: the frigate. Fast-moving and extremely manoeuvrable, these vessels were the 'eyes of the fleet', used for reconnaissance, message-carrying and, where appropriate, to harass the enemy in minor actions. They were fifth-raters, carrying between 32 and 44 guns, and they carried a complement of around 300, including Marines.

TASK FORCE

The eighteenth-century conflicts in which Britain was involved saw the increasing use of Royal Navy vessels as part of what would nowadays be called a 'task force', carrying troops to distant waters and supporting them in subsequent land operations. One of the most ambitious was mounted in March 1741, when 126 ships carrying eight regiments of Royal Marines, as well as soldiers from England and the colonies, assembled off Cartagena, on the northern coast of what is now Colombia. Cartagena was the strongest fortress on the Spanish Main, and it had never been taken.

Admiral Edward Vernon, commanding the fleet – the largest that had ever been assembled in American waters – had plenty of men to do the job, but he was faced with a logistical nightmare. The fleet covered miles of sea, and it was five days before all Vernon's captains had even received their individual orders. Nevertheless, the troops were disembarked, aware that the delay had given the Spaniards time to strengthen their defences. But it was yellow fever, rather than powder and shot, that defeated the attackers; hundreds died in the assault, but thousands died of disease, and there was no alternative but to re-embark the survivors. After six weeks, the operation was called off and the fleet sailed away.

It was during the course of what became known as the Seven Years War (1756–63) that the Royal Navy reached a high peak of renown, revealing as never before the value of maritime strategy in the struggle for empire. Wolfe's success in capturing Quebec in September 1759, for example, could never have been achieved without the support of the Royal Navy, whose ships navigated the treacherous St Lawrence river in the face of all manner of difficulties, and whose Royal Marines fought shoulder to shoulder with the army on the Heights of Abraham. The campaign saw the use of flat-bottomed assault craft, each carrying 50 or 60 men. The era of amphibious warfare, and of combined operations, had begun.

In 1759, Admiral Lord Hawke, flying his flag in the *Royal George*, won a resounding victory over the French at Quiberon Bay, on the Bay of Biscay. The flagship of the French rear-admiral was shot to pieces and she struck her colours after suffering appalling casualties; a 74-gun ship foundered in the heavy sea; and another was sunk after broadsides had holed her near the waterline. Several other ships ran aground and were destroyed. They included the French flagship, *Soleil Royal*, which was abandoned and set on fire by her crew.

Quiberon Bay was the Royal Navy's third major victory in four months, and Britain now enjoyed undisputed supremacy on the high seas. After 1759, France lost one overseas colony after another – Dominica, Guadaloupe and Martinique in the Caribbean, Calcutta and Pondicherry in India – and when Spain entered the war on France's side, the British wrested Manila and Havana from her. These colonies were returned to their previous owners when peace was signed in 1763, with a notable exception: Britain kept Canada.

The years of conflict with the American colonies, from 1775 to 1783, involved renewed warfare with both France and Spain. During this period there were four main areas of operations: the English Channel and its approaches, the West Indies and east coast of North America, the Far East, and Gibraltar. It was off the Americas that the principal naval engagements were fought, and one of them changed the course of the War of Independence.

It happened in September 1781, when the British Admiral Graves, whose ships were carrying supplies for the army of

General Cornwallis, came upon a French naval force under Admiral de Grasse in Chesapeake Bay. After an indecisive action, very poorly conducted by Graves, the latter had to withdraw to repair damage. The result was that Cornwallis, starved of provisions and with no naval support, was forced to surrender.

NAVAL VICTORIES

On the credit side, a naval task force under the ageing Admiral Sir George Rodney was despatched to relieve Gibraltar, which was under siege by the Spaniards, before proceeding to the West Indies. Setting out on 8 January 1780, he came upon a Spanish convoy off Finisterre, comprising 15 merchant vessels escorted by five armed ships, and captured all of them. Sending the warships back to England with prize crews, Rodney took the merchantmen – which were mostly laden with wheat and flour – on with him towards Gibraltar.

A week later, on 16 January, Rodney had another stroke of luck when he encountered 11 Spanish ships of the line under Don Juan de Langara, deployed to intercept Gibraltar-bound supply convoys. The Spaniards ran for harbour in tempestuous weather, but Rodney's ships overhauled them and a running fight began, lasting well into the night. One ship, the 70-gun *San Domingo*, blew up with the loss of 600 men; four others, of 80 guns, struck their colours; and two more of 70 guns ran aground and were lost. Of the original 11 ships in the Spanish fleet, only four of them succeeded in reaching the safety of the port of Cadiz.

In 1793, war was declared against the infant French Republic by a powerful consortium of nations led by Britain. It continued for 22 years, and saw the Royal Navy rise to the peak of its power in the age of sail. The period is remembered for a series of great naval victories over the French, culminating in the Battle of Trafalgar in 1805. In fact there were only four major engagements against the French, including Trafalgar, and most of the Royal Navy's time was occupied with unglamorous and boring convoy escort and blockade duty. Yet the fleet engagements that were fought were conducted with great skill and discipline, and made the admirals involved into almost legendary heroes.

The first big naval battle of the period occurred as the result of a desperate attempt by the French to ship grain to France, which was on the verge of starvation following a bad harvest in 1793. A large amount of grain was purchased in America and loaded into a convoy of 125 ships, and 26 warships of the Brest Squadron, commanded by Admiral Louis Thomas Villaret de Joyeuse, were ordered to sea to provide the escort on the final stage of the journey.

The British Admiralty, having learned of the convoy, ordered Admiral Earl 'Black Dick' Howe to intercept it. He put to sea with 34 ships of the line and 15 frigates, but had to detach eight to escort a British convoy bound for America, so

BELOW: The Battle of the Nile fought at Aboukir Bay in 1798. This decisive victory ended Napoleon's, and France's, ambitions towards the east.

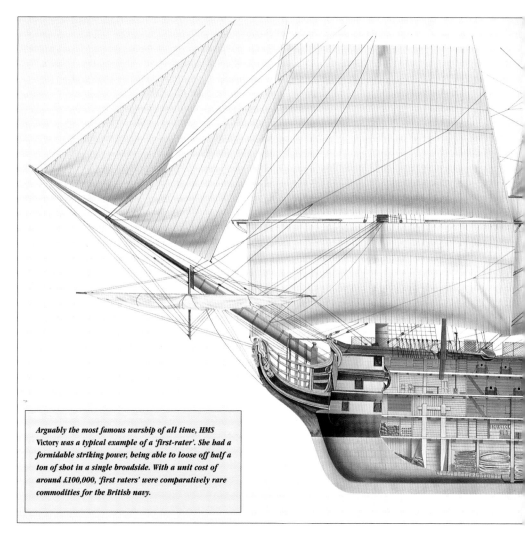

Arguably the most famous warship of all time, HMS Victory was a typical example of a 'first-rater'. She had a formidable striking power, being able to loose off half a ton of shot in a single broadside. With a unit cost of around £100,000, 'first raters' were comparatively rare commodities for the British navy.

that both sides were evenly matched. Howe had three first-raters of 100 guns, including his flagship *Queen Charlotte*, four 98-gunners, two 80-gunners, and 17 74-gunners. The French fleet included Villaret de Joyeuse's huge flagship *Montagne* with 120 guns, three 100-gunners, including the *Republicain* and *Revolutionnaire* (formerly the *Royal Louis* and *Bretagne*), four 80-gunners and 18 74-gunners.

On 28 May 1794, Howe caught up with the French 400 miles west of Ushant. Battle was joined in the evening after a lengthy chase. The *Revolutionnaire* was badly damaged, and had to be towed into Rochefort; but HMS *Audacious* also suffered severely and had to retire from the fleet. The action

resumed the next morning, Howe ordering his ships to break through the enemy's line. Although the *Queen Charlotte* succeeded in doing so, many of Howe's captains did not see signal in the smoke of battle and the manoeuvre was not successful, the French managing to reform.

Dense fog brought about a lull in the fighting on 30–31 May. By an extraordinary coincidence, a merchant ship with Howe's youngest daughter on board, in passage from Lisbon to Ireland, sailed right through the French fleet without its crew realising the enemy ships were there.

When the fog cleared on the morning of 1 June, the two fleets were still in sight of one another and the British

attacked in line, led by *Caesar* and then *Bellerophon*. *Queen Charlotte* was in the centre of the column, with HMS *Thunderer* bringing up the rear. Once again, Howe ordered his ships to break the enemy line. The *Queen Charlotte* executed the manoeuvre perfectly, passing between *Montagne*'s stern and *Jacobin*'s bow, raking both. The line was also broken by the *Leviathan, Russell, Marlborough, Defence, Brunswick, Ramillies* and *Royal George*. The *Brunswick* engaged the *Vengeur du Peuple* (74 guns) which sank after a three-hour duel, many of her crew being rescued by British seamen at great risk to themselves.

The battle began at about 0930 hours. At 1013 hours, with the French line losing its cohesion and ships beginning to break away, Howe signalled 'general chase'. Villaret de Joyeuse, however, managed to extricate 19 of his ships, five of which had to be towed away. Six French ships (two 80-gunners and four 74-gunners) were captured. Howe's fleet had also suffered badly, 11 ships sustaining severe damage to their rigging and two (*Defence* and *Marlborough*) being completely dismasted. The British suffered 90 killed and 858 wounded; total French casualties, including prisoners, were 7500.

In one sense this battle – which became known as the 'Glorious First of June' – was a failure in that the French grain convoy got through. But it vindicated the tactic of breaking the line, which was to be used by the Royal Navy with

resounding success in subsequent actions against a variety of foes.

CAPE ST VINCENT

In August 1796, Spain allied herself with France, forcing the British Mediterranean Fleet, commanded by Admiral Sir John Jervis, to evacuate its bases in Corsica and Elba and move to Gibraltar, from where it transferred its operations to the Atlantic. On 14 February 1797, a scouting frigate reported to Jervis, who was lying off Cape St Vincent, near Cadiz, that a

Spanish force of unknown strength was approaching. Jervis had 15 ships of the line at his disposal, including two of 100 guns. One was the *Britannia*; the other, his own flagship, had been in service for nearly two decades, having been commissioned in 1778. Her name was HMS *Victory*. He also had two 98-gunners, two 90-gunners, eight 74-gunners and one 64-gunner, HMS *Diadem*. One of the 74-gunners, HMS *Captain*, was commanded by an officer whose name would soon be linked with that of HMS *Victory* in unquenchable glory. He was Commodore Horatio Nelson.

It was HMS *Victory*'s Captain Calder who advised Jervis, by signal, of the numbers of enemy ships that crept over the horizon: eight at first, then 20, then 25. At that, Jervis stopped the count, stating that if there were 50 he would still engage them. In fact there were 27, led by Admiral Jose de Cordoba in the mighty 136-gun *Santissima Trinidad*, the largest warship afloat. The Spanish fleet included six ships of 112 guns, two of 84 and 18 74-gunners, so that the Spaniards had a theoretical superiority of 2308 guns to Jervis's 1232. But Cordoba's crews were of a poor standard and his ships were not in battle formation, being widely separated in two groups.

Seizing the tactical advantage, Jervis arranged his fleet into one long column and sailed between the two enemy groups, engaging the larger one of 19 ships. Cordoba, attempting to avoid an engagement, tried to outrun the British by making off on a reciprocal heading to Jervis's column, which reversed its course too late. It was Nelson, third from the rear of the British line, who spotted the danger and broke away on his own initiative, attacking the head of the Spanish fleet. He was closely followed by his friend Commodore Cuthbert Collingwood, commanding the rearmost ship, HMS *Excellent*.

A raging battle began at about 1330 hours, Nelson's HMS *Captain* engaging the Spanish flagship while Collingwood attacked the 112-gun *Salvador del Mundo* and then the 74-gun *San Ysidro*, which struck her colours. Collingwood then turned to assist Nelson, whose ship had been partially dismasted, and HMS *Culloden*, having tacked, raced back from her position at the head of the line for the same purpose. Nelson's HMS *Captain* was now grappling with the *San Nicolas*, and he stormed her at the head of a boarding party and captured her. The Spanish *San Josef* had become entangled with the *San Nicolas* while manoeuvring to avoid HMS *Culloden*, so Nelson's party rushed on across the deck of the *San Nicolas* and took the other ship as well.

The *Santissima Trinidad*, meanwhile, had a lucky escape. Under savage attack by the *Orion*, *Irresistible* and *Excellent*, she had actually lowered her colours when the remainder of the Spanish fleet came up to her rescue, enabling her to limp away. But the *Salvador del Mundo* struck and was captured, whereupon Jervis decided to abandon the action and reform his line.

MARITIME ENEMY

The Spaniards, in addition to losing four ships, had three more so badly damaged that they were unfit to fight, and Cordoba's flagship was little more than a floating wreck. He therefore decided not to renew the battle, and took the remnants of his fleet into Cadiz. Including prisoners, he had lost some 2800 men. British losses were 73 killed and 227 wounded, with five ships damaged.

Jervis, although criticised for not pursuing the Spaniards, was awarded an earldom for his action off Cape St Vincent. Yet, in truth, it was Horatio Nelson and Cuthbert Collingwood who had brought about the victory.

There was little doubt that, at the close of the eighteenth century, the most redoubtable maritime enemy Britain had to face was Holland, whose fleet – in alliance with those of France and Spain – formed a serious invasion threat. Dutch seamen were every bit as good as their British counterparts,

ABOVE: Nelson's cabin on HMS Victory, *with the writing desk at which he penned his last letters before the battle. Before an engagement, valuable furniture was stored on towed boats.*

and keeping their ships blockaded in port was the vital responsibility of the North Sea Fleet under the command of a large and fierce Scot, Admiral Adam Duncan.

In October 1797, the Dutch fleet sailed out of the Texel with the intention of joining the French fleet and making a landing in Ireland. Early on 11 October, the Dutch were sighted off Kamperduin (Camperdown), north of Haarlem, by Duncan's force, which consisted of 16 ships of the line (seven 74-gunners, including his flagship HMS *Venerable*, seven 64-gunners and two 50-gunners). The Dutch fleet, commanded by Admiral Jan Willem de Winter comprised 17 ships of the line (four 74-gunners, including the flagship *Vrijheid*, five 68-gunners, two 64-gunners, four 56-gunners and two 44-gunners), as well as eight frigates. De Winter formed his fleet into two lines, with the big warships nearest to the British and the frigates out on the flank. Duncan attacked in two columns, intent on cutting through the enemy line, and at about 1230 hours, battle was joined when the column led by Admiral Onslow's HMS *Monarch*, with 74 guns, cut the Dutch line three ships from the rear. The four Dutch ships at this end of the line, heavily outnumbered, were soon overwhelmed and captured, as was the 44-gun frigate *Monnikendam*, which tried to assist them.

Fifteen minutes after the battle broke, Duncan's column smashed through the Dutch line five ships from its head and HMS *Venerable* engaged de Winter's *Vrijheid*, precipitating a furious mêlée which, for two hours, saw *Venerable* in combat with four Dutch vessels until HMS *Ardent*, herself badly damaged and with many casualties, came to her aid.

At about 1430 hours, with other British ships – including
Captain Bligh's HMS _Director_ – bearing down upon him, de
Winter saw the results of the battle at the rear of the column
and decided to strike his colours, whereupon the battle
ended. Eleven Dutch ships were captured, with over 1000
casualties, including prisoners. British losses were 203 killed
and 622 wounded.

With the Dutch fleet effectively destroyed and the threat
from that quarter removed, the focus of naval operations
now switched to the Mediterranean, where much activity
had been observed in the ports of southern France. A large
naval squadron under Horatio Nelson, now a rear-admiral,
was dispatched to investigate. In May 1798, a French fleet of
72 warships of all types, plus 400 transports carrying 35,000
troops, sailed for Egypt undetected by Nelson, who was
hampered by bad weather and a lack of frigates for reconnaissance. He instituted a search, but the French eluded him,
and on 1 July they arrived at Alexandria, where they disembarked their troops.

Nelson's ongoing search brought him to Alexandria a
month later. Although there were transports in the harbour,
there was no sign of the French battle fleet which was his
principal objective; it was located shortly afterwards at
Aboukir Bay, in the Nile delta. The French commander,
Admiral Francois Paul Brueys d'Aigaillers, had anchored his
ships in a line a short distance from shore, protected by
shoals and a shore battery. His fleet numbered 13 ships of
the line, including his flagship, the big 120-gun _L'Orient_,
three 80-gunners (_Franklin_, _Tonnant_ and _Guillaume Tell_), three
80-gunners and nine 74-gunners. Four frigates were
anchored in a second line closer in towards the shore.

Nelson had 14 ships of the line, but nothing larger than a
74-gunner; his flagship was HMS _Vanguard_. He decided to
attack immediately, but as he approached the French fleet
the 74-gun HMS _Culloden_ – a veteran of the 'Glorious First of
June' and Cape St Vincent battles – ran aground on a
sandbank, so that both fleets were now equal in numbers.

FURIOUS CANNONADE

Leading the attack in HMS _Goliath_, Captain Thomas Foley
took the bold step of breaking through and positioning himself between the two lines of enemy ships, bombarding the
ships of the line from the landward side and taking them by
surprise. Two or three other vessels followed suit, but by the
time Nelson's _Vanguard_ and the remainder of the British fleet
came up it was growing dusk, so Nelson led his ships down
the enemy's seaward side, subjecting them to a furious can-
nonade. The fight was not all one-sided; HMS _Bellerophon_,
severely battered and dismasted, drifted away with 49 of her
crew dead and 148 wounded.

With the light fading fast, three more British ships entered the battle. They were the *Leander*, which had gone to the assistance of the grounded *Culloden*, the *Alexander* and the *Swiftsure*. Captain Thomas Thompson of the *Leander* spotted a gap in the French line left by the *Peuple Souverain*, which had drifted clear when her anchor cable was severed by a shot, and passed through to attack the *Franklin* and the flagship, *L'Orient*.

Both admirals were now wounded. Nelson had been struck above his sightless eye by an iron splinter but remained in command, despite being in shock and great pain; but Brueys was in a far worse state, having lost both legs. Yet he too continued to direct his crew until a ball from HMS *Swiftsure* ended his life.

L'Orient was now blazing fiercely and Brueys's Chief of Staff, Admiral Ganteaume, gave the order to abandon ship. At about 2200 hours, the flagship blew up in a tremendous explosion that momentarily stopped the battle. It must have come as a merciful release to her wounded, who had been left to burn below decks. Among those who perished was Brueys's young son, who had stayed beside his father until the end – a gallant and sacrificial act that inspired the poet Felicia Hemans to write her famous work 'The Boy Stood on the Burning Deck'.

Of the French fleet that had anchored at Aboukir, only two ships of the line – the *Guillaume Tell* and *Le Generaux* – escaped, along with two frigates. Of the other 10, one had blown up and nine were captured. French casualties were around 1700 dead; the British lost over 200 killed and a further 700 wounded. It was a small price to pay for achieving the most decisive naval victory of the eighteenth century, and one that dashed Napoleon Bonaparte's dreams of oriental conquest for ever.

Early in 1801, a British fleet of 20 ships of the line and 30 smaller vessels, under Admiral Sir Hyde Parker with Nelson as his second-in-command, sailed for the Baltic in a show of force designed to persuade Denmark to pull out of the so-called 'Armed Neutrality of the North,' a pact between Russia, Denmark, Sweden and Prussia that had been formed to stop British warships stopping and searching neutral vessels suspected of carrying contraband cargoes to France. Diplomatic negotiations broke down, and a week later the fleet bore down on Copenhagen, where the Danes had set up impressive defences. There were eight blockships, of which seven were ships of the line with between 52 and 74 guns and one a former merchantman with 26; five floating batteries with between 18 and 24 guns; one unrigged 74-gunner, the *Saelland*; two fully rigged ships of the line (*Trekroner* with 74 guns, and *Danmark* with 70 guns); two flat barges, each mounting 22 guns; a six-gun corvette; two

18-gun brigs; a 20-gun transport; two frigates of 22 and 40 guns; and 11 gunboats, each with four guns. In addition there were the formidable defences of the Trekroner and Lynetten Forts, commanding the approaches to the Naval Harbour.

Parker, reluctant to commit his larger ships in case they ran aground, ordered Nelson to attack with 12 ships of the line and some support vessels. He decided to lead the assault in the 74-gun HMS *Elephant*, to which he transferred his flag from the 98-gun *Goliath*. His squadron comprised seven 74-gunners, three 64-gunners, one 56-gunner, one 50-gunner, six frigates, three brigs, seven bomb-ketches and two fire-ships. The 56-gunner was Captain William Bligh's *Glatton*, which was armed entirely with carronades – close-range guns firing balls of between 17.25 and 30.8kg (38 and 68 pounds).

BLIND EYE

At first light on 2 April 1801, Nelson launched his attack on the moored defences and almost immediately encountered trouble when three of his ships, the *Russell* (74 guns), *Bellona* (74 guns) and *Agamemnon* (64 guns) ran aground. At about 1030 hours, the nine remaining ships of the line opened fire on their selected targets and the frigates engaged the

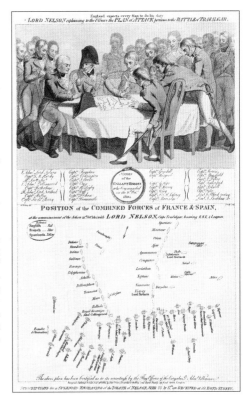

Trekroner batteries. The Danish commander, Johan Fischer, was forced to abandon the blockship *Dannebroge* when she was set on fire; he transferred his flag to the *Holstein*, only to make another enforced move to the Trekroner Fort when that ship surrendered.

At about 1300 hours, just when Nelson was gaining the upper hand, Admiral Parker signalled him to break off the action, having been informed that three ships were aground and believing that victory was no longer possible.

Nelson's response passed into naval legend; he placed his telescope to his blind eye, claiming that he could not see Parker's signal, and ordered his captains to engage the enemy more closely. By this time, eight Danish ships had been wrecked or captured, and after another hour only three remained in combat. Yet the Danes fought on with great gallantry; the 58-gun blockship *Provensteen* only surrendered after 56 of her guns had been put out of action.

Nelson proposed a truce, which was accepted. The loss of life on both sides was appalling; the Danes suffered 1035 casualties, the British 944. But the destruction of the Danish fleet effectively brought an end to the Armed Neutrality

LEFT: The whole nation mourned the death of Admiral Lord Nelson. The Battle of Trafalgar meant that France and Spain would never more present a threat to Britain on the High Seas.

ABOVE: The Duke of Wellington, a sailing ship, was hastily fitted with engines in 1852. It would be another 30 years before sails completely disappeared from warships in favour of engine power.

pact, and with it an end to the threat to British trade in the Baltic, on which the Royal Navy depended for supplies of timber, pitch and other materials. The Peace of Amiens (March 1802) brought a temporary lull in hostilities between France and England, but it was no more than an armed truce. The British Government knew very well that Napoleon's preparations for war were continuing, and the conflict resumed in May 1803. By this time the French has assembled a colossal army of 100,000 men – the 'Army of England' – with its centre on Boulogne; 50,000 more were encamped on either wing, from Brest on the one hand, to Antwerp on the other. The assembly of a vast number of invasion barges left the British in no doubt about Napoleon's intention.

First, the French had to seize control of the English Channel, if only temporarily. Since the French fleet had little chance of defeating the Royal Navy, the obvious solution was for the French to lure the British fleet away, then make a swift return to embark the Army of England. On 29 March 1805, the French fleet, under Admiral Pierre de Villeneuve, slipped out of Toulon and, avoiding Nelson's patrols under cover of bad weather, joined up with a Spanish fleet under Admiral the Duke of Gravina. The combined force then sailed for the West Indies, followed belatedly by Nelson, who had lost time searching for them in the Mediterranean.

With 18 ships of the line, seven of them Spanish, Villeneuve arrived at Martinique on 14 May, three days after Nelson had begun his pursuit across the Atlantic. Villeneuve expected to meet the rest of the French fleet there, under Admiral Ganteaume; but Napoleon had ordered the latter to remain in Brest until an opportunity arose to sneak out past the British blockade. It never did.

THE SHIPS OF NELSON'S BATTLE FLEET

FIRST-RATER. These vessels mounted 100 or more cannon ranging from 12-pounders to 32-pounders. They measured over 61m (200ft) on the lower gun deck and were generally crewed by 875 officers and men. Their unit cost was huge for its day – about £100,000 – which accounted for the fact that fewer than a dozen were in service at any one time. A first-rater could loose off half a ton of iron shot in a single broadside.
Examples: *Victory*, *Royal Sovereign*, *Britannia*.

SECOND-RATER. Only slightly less impressive than the first-rater, this vessel carried 90 to 98 cannon on three gun decks, the lower one of which was 59m (195ft) long. A second-rater was manned by 750–800 men.
Examples: *Dreadnought*, *Prince*.

THIRD-RATER. This ship of the line came in several sizes, from 80-gun three-deckers to 64-gun two-deckers. Crew was between 490 and 720. Third-raters accounted for the bulk of the Royal Navy's battle fleet at the time of Trafalgar – 147 out of a total of 175 capital ships.
Examples: *Neptune* (80), *Bellerophon* (74), *Thunderer* (74), *Africa* (64).

FOURTH-RATER. These 45m (150ft) vessels were two-deckers, mounting between 50 and 56 guns. Crewed by 350 officers and men, their main role was as flagships of cruiser squadrons serving overseas.
Example: *Calcutta*

FIFTH-RATER. These 45m (150ft) frigates, with a crew of 250 and a single gun deck, were the 'eyes' of the fleet, scouting ahead for contact with the enemy. They also made excellent commerce raiders. They mounted 32–40 guns on a single deck.
Examples: *Sirius*, *Phoebe*, *Mars*.

SIXTH-RATER. These ships were nimble sloops, 38m (125ft) long with a crew of about 195. Their speed and manoeuvrability made them very useful escort vessels, and they were also used as fast couriers.
Example: *Pickle*.

Receiving news that Nelson had reached the West Indies, Villeneuve decided to sail back across the Atlantic. Five days later Nelson followed him, sending his fastest frigate, the *Curieux* (Captain Bettesworth) to carry intelligence of the enemy's movements to England. On receiving the news, the First Sea Lord, Admiral Lord Barham, took immediate steps to strengthen Britain's defences and sent part of the Channel Fleet, under Admiral Sir Robert Calder, to patrol the Biscay approaches. On 22 July, Calder came upon Villeneuve's force off Cape Finisterre, and in a brief and foggy engagement he succeeded in capturing two of the seven Spanish ships which had accompanied Villeneuve to the West Indies.

Villeneuve slipped away in the fog and on 1 August reached Ferrol, where he set about repairing his ships and tending his sick, of which there were many. About 1000 had already been offloaded at Martinique and Dominica. Twelve days later, in response to Napoleon's urging, he re-emerged and sailed for the Channel, where 30 British men-of-war blocked his path. Mistaking the lights of a merchant convoy for those of British warships, Villeneuve turned south and headed for Cadiz. Admiral Sir Cuthbert Collingwood, who was blockading the port, let him pass into harbour without hindrance and then slammed the door shut on him, leaving frigates on patrol and sailing to join Nelson.

The latter, who had reached Europe two days before Villeneuve (the Royal Navy's ships were faster, having copper-sheathed bottoms that kept marine growths at bay, and were far better handled than the enemy's) had put to sea from Gibraltar and was now on station off Cape Trafalgar. On 19 October, Villeneuve, now commanding a combined Franco-Spanish fleet of 33 ships of the line, put to sea again and headed south, intending to enter the Mediterranean and attack Malta's supply routes.

GENERAL CHASE

This time, there was no element of surprise. The nimble frigate *Euryalus*, patrolling off Cadiz, signalled the enemy's exit from harbour to her sister *Phoebe*, who in turn signalled it to *Mars*. Mars, in turn, sped the news to HMS *Victory*, Nelson's flagship, and aloft the signal fluttered from *Victory* to the fleet: 'General Chase. Southeast.'

Eighteen of the enemy's ships of the line were French (four 80-gunners and the rest 74-gunners) and 15 Spanish. Flagship of the Spanish force was the mighty 130-gun *Santissima Trinidad*; there were also two 112-gunners, one 100-gunner, two 80-gunners and one 64-gunner, the remainder being 74-gunners.

Against this array, Nelson had 27 ships of the line, including three 100-gunners, four 98-gunners, one 80-gunner, three 64-gunners, and the rest were 74-gunners. In an extension of the tactic of cutting the enemy's line, Nelson planned to attack in three columns in line ahead, to overwhelm the enemy's rear and centre before the van could reverse its course and come to their aid. The outcome, Nelson expected, would be a 'pell-mell battle which would surprise and confound the enemy', permitting the superior British gunnery and ship-handling to be exploited to maximum effect. In the event, only two columns were formed. They were to prove enough.

The battle began shortly after noon on 21 October, when the leeward column, led by Admiral Collingwood's 100-gun *Royal Sovereign*, broke the Franco-Spanish line and was soon heavily engaged – Collingwood's flagship battled with five enemy vessels at one point. Within an hour Nelson's windward column was also in action. HMS *Victory*, followed by *Temeraire*, *Neptune* and *Britannia*, passed astern of Villeneuve's flagship *Bucentaure*, which she battered at point-blank range, causing fearsome casualties among her crew. Then *Victory* was herself engaged by the French *Redoutable* and the two giants poured salvo after salvo into one another, lying entangled while sharpshooters poured down a rain of musket fire from overhead. At about 1330 hours, a French sharpshooter saw Admiral Nelson on *Victory*'s quarterdeck, clearly identified by the tarnished stars and ribbons on his uniform, and brought him down with a ball that entered his shoulder and lodged in his spine.

Nelson died at 1630 hours, comforted by the knowledge that victory was his. By the time the leading enemy ships had reversed their course, their centre and rear had been overwhelmed. The shattered *Bucentaure* had surrendered, Villeneuve was a prisoner, and eighteen other enemy vessels, including the *Santissima Trinidad*, had struck their colours. Those enemy ships that could, headed for the coast; one was the French ship of the line *Achille*, which caught fire and exploded at about 1730 hours.

The British lost some 450 men killed and 1100 wounded at Trafalgar. The combined Franco-Spanish loss, killed and wounded, was about 14,000, many of these being drowned when their ships were wrecked by fierce storms that swept across Biscay for a week after the battle. No British ships were lost in the terrible weather, but it was a sorry-looking fleet that assembled in Gibraltar; the *Victory*, which had been almost completely dismasted, had to be towed into harbour by HMS *Neptune*.

ABOVE: **It was ironic that warships, which by the late eighteenth century had become awesome killing machines, should also feature ornate decorative carvings.**

Nelson's victory at Trafalgar did not save England from the threat of an immediate invasion, as has sometimes been supposed. Napoleon had already abandoned his invasion plans by October 1805, and had set his face towards the east as Adolf Hitler would do over a century later. But the destruction of the combined Franco-Spanish fleet meant that his maritime power was crushed once and for all, so that no future invasion could be contemplated.

To the Lords of the Admiralty, it must have seemed, after the Battle of Trafalgar, that the mighty men-of-war of Britain's navy were invincible, and that these stout hulls of oak, crowned with their dazzling white sails, would remain the symbols of British sea power for evermore. They were to be proved wrong.

CHAPTER 2

STEEL AND STEAM

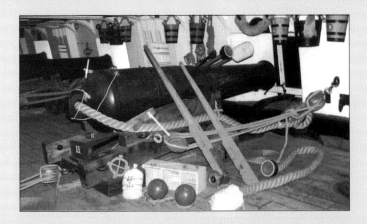

A decade after the Battle of Trafalgar, while most senior officers were of the firm belief that Britain's 'wooden walls' would rule the seas forever, a revolution was under way which would sweep them all aside before many more years had passed. The age of steel and steam was dawning.

She was called the *Charlotte Dundas*, and in 1801 she towed barges on the Forth and Clyde Canal. She was quite unremarkable, except for one thing. She was the first successful steamship in the world.

Steamship development might have progressed at a faster rate had it not been for the war with Napoleon. But in 1812 the *Comet* started a passenger steamship service on the Clyde,

ABOVE: Manned by a crew of 18 men, the 68pdr – seen here mounted in HMS Warrior (1860) – was the Royal Navy's favourite gun, capable of smashing through armour with deadly effect.

LEFT: The 'Royal Sovereigns' of the 1880s were a highly successful design and were faster than any contemporary battleships. They were armed with four 324mm (13.5in) guns in barbettes.

and two years later the *Margery*, also built on the Clyde, sailed down the east coast to London, to begin a similar service on the Thames. In 1816, the first Channel crossing was made by a steamboat, the *Elise*, and in 1818 a regular steamship service was inaugurated between Greenock, on the Clyde, and Belfast.

After that, progress was swift. In 1825 the 477-tonne (470-ton) *Enterprise* reached Calcutta from England in 113 days, using steam for two-thirds of the voyage; and in 1827 the *Curacao*, built in Dover and sold to the Dutch navy, began a series of crossings from Holland to the West Indies.

Apart from hiring steam tugs to tow warships out of harbour in the 1820s when the winds were unfavourable, the Royal Navy showed no interest in steam. For one thing, it was argued that the Royal Navy had commitments

worldwide – the use of steamships would mean setting up coaling stations at strategic points, shipping the fuel out to them, and defending them.

One man, more than any other, was responsible for persuading the Admiralty to change its mind. He was the engineer Isambard Kingdom Brunel, designer of the three great commercial steamships of the mid-nineteenth century: the *Great Western*, *Great Eastern* and *Great Britain*. The *Great Britain* was the most innovative of the three, and among the innovations was a screw propeller instead of a paddle wheel. The idea was not Brunel's – a screw propeller had already been patented and, in 1838, tested on a small ship called the *Archimedes*, named after the Greek inventor of the screw for raising water in about 200BC.

Despite teething troubles, which included the break-up of her first propeller, the *Great Britain* – an iron ship 98m (322ft) long, nearly half the length again of any warship afloat – made four trips to New York.

Brunel wrote a lengthy report on the screw propeller while the *Great Britain* was on the stocks. It was examined by Admiralty officials, who realized that the use of a propeller would eliminate one of the principal objections to steam-powered warships, which was that a paddle wheel would get in the way of a ship's broadside gun arrangement. With advice from Brunel, the Admiralty authorized the building of a small screw-driven steam sloop, the *Rattler*, for use as a trials ship. In 1845 she was matched against a paddle steamer of similar size and won easily, ending the test by towing the paddle steamer backwards.

After that, new warships were designed with engines and propellers, and some older vessels were retrofitted, but the engines were for auxiliary power only; sail remained the main source of power, and many senior naval officers were dead-set against change. It was the Crimean War that forced the issue. Although the Russians had no navy capable of confronting the British, the latter quickly discovered, during naval bombardment operations in the Black Sea and the Baltic, that ships with engines were far more useful and manoeuvrable than those with just sails when it came to evading counter-fire from shore batteries.

GUNBOATS

It was the Crimean War that nurtured the Royal Navy's 'gunboat diplomacy'. Throughout Victorian times, the gunboat was a principal instrument in policing the empire. Almost 200 were built in 1855–56, all 30–36m (100–120ft) long, with engines of 20–60hp and a full rig of sail, mounting a 68-pounder gun forward, a 32-pounder aft, and two 24-pounders amidships. They carried a crew of 30 or 40, commanded by a lieutenant, an ideal first command for an ambitious young officer in a navy where chances of promotion had hitherto often depended on the death of someone more senior.

In 1848 the French launched the *Napoleon*, the first steam-powered battleship. Two years later Britain made a response of sorts by producing the *Agamemnon*, which, as a sailing ship with an auxiliary engine, was no real comparison; but in 1853 the British launched the *Duke of Wellington*, which resembled the *Napoleon* and had a 2000hp engine. The next step in what was fast becoming a naval arms race was taken when the French introduced explosive shells instead of cannon balls, and built a ship capable of withstanding such missiles. She was the *Gloire*, based on the design of the *Napoleon*, and she carried battery armour of 110–120mm (4.3–4.7in). Begun in 1858, she was the first armoured ship-of-the-line in the world.

Britain's answer was the *Warrior* of 1859, a vessel superior in most respects to the *Gloire*. The was the first seagoing iron-hulled armoured warship, having 114mm (4.5in) of wrought iron on a backing of 457mm (18in) of teak. She started her career with an armament of breech-loading guns of various calibres, but the breech mechanism was prone to failure, with disastrous results for the gun crews. In 1867, the armament was changed to 28 178mm (7in) and four 203mm (8in) muzzle-loaders. She carried a complement of 707 and had a displacement of 9358 tonnes (9210 tons). She had a sister ship, the *Black Prince*, launched in 1861.

By 1869, 38 steam-powered capital ships were either in service with, or under construction for, the Royal Navy. The earlier designs were broadside ironclads, but 1864 saw the launch of the 3942-tonne (3880-ton) *Prince Albert*, which had

single 230mm (4.9in) guns mounted in four turrets on the centreline. Other ships had their guns mounted in a central battery. But all carried sails, and it was not until 1868 that Britain laid down a seagoing vessel designed to be powered by steam alone.

MAJOR DISASTER

She was the *Devastation*, and her concept was much reviled by the traditionalists in navy circles. Completed in 1873, she carried four 305mm (12in) muzzle-loading guns mounted in turrets and was powered by direct-acting trunk engines, with eight rectangular boilers and two screws. She displaced 9480 tonnes (9330 tons) and had a complement of 358. Her sister ship was the *Thunderer*.

Much more satisfying to the orthodox naval mind was the *Captain*, completed in 1870. She was also a turret ship, dis-placing 7892 tonnes (7767 tons) and her machinery was similar to that of the *Devastation*. But she carried a full rig of sail, and she had a serious flaw. Because overweight material was used in her construction, she floated too deeply, having a freeboard of only 2m (6ft 6in) instead of the designed 2.6m (8ft 6in) – already low in itself. On 7 September 1870, only nine months after she was completed, she capsized and sank in a Biscay gale, taking 473 of her crew – including her designer, Captain Cowper Coles – with her. It had taken a major disaster to end the chapter of naval sailing ships.

Although the naval gun turret was now a fact of life, it was not until the late 1870s that the Royal Navy returned to the breech-loading concept. The first British battleships to feature breech-loading turret-mounted guns were the *Colossus* and the *Edinburgh*. Both were laid down in 1879 but took 10

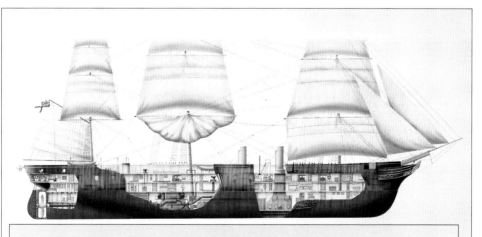

The Warrior, *pictured here, and her sister vessel* Black Prince *were the first seagoing iron-hulled armoured warships, and were built to overtake and destroy any other warship.*

Ships like HMS Victoria of the 1850s were hybrids. Their principle source of power was the wind, with engines – still deeply mistrusted – acting as an auxiliary source. They retained the gun ports of their all-sail predecessors.

years to complete, the work being held up by delays in the delivery of their armament. They mounted four 305mm (12in) guns in two central turrets amidships, together with a secondary armament of five 152mm (6in) guns. They displaced 9297 tonnes (9150 tons) and had a complement of 396. They were also the first British battleships to have compound armour instead of iron.

It was the *Collingwood*, however, laid down in 1880, that set a trend in British battleship design that would endure for a quarter of a century. Her main armament of four 305mm (12in) guns were mounted in twin barbettes fore and aft, a concept originally developed by the French. The barbette

consisted of a turntable mounted inside a short, vertical circular tube, the guns firing over a low-armoured parapet. Early barbettes lacked overhead protection, but this was added later.

The 'Admiral' class barbette battleships *Anson*, *Benbow*, *Camperdown*, *Howe* and *Rodney*, also constructed during the

RIGHT: The **Prince Albert** *of 1862 was the first British turret ship. She had an iron hull and carried four gun turrets on the centreline. She spent most of her career in reserve.*

ABOVE: With no sail power, masts or rigging, HMS Devastation of 1868 was generally condemned at the time. Yet she performed well, and was a revolutionary design. She served until 1907.

1880s, carried a heavy armament of four 343mm (13.5in) and six 152mm (6in) guns, as well as a variety of smaller weapons. The exception was the *Benbow*, whose main armament comprised two 413mm (16.25in) guns. They carried heavy armour, too, their belt being up to 457mm (18in) and the barbettes 355mm (14in). The increase was made possible by the growing use of mild steel in place of wrought iron. The *Camperdown* of this class achieved a certain notoriety on 22 June 1893 when she accidentally rammed and sank the battleship *Victoria*, flagship of Vice-Admiral Sir George Tryon, off the coast of Syria with the loss of 358 lives, including Tryon's, out of a complement of 430. The *Victoria* had only been completed in 1890 and was the first battleship with triple expansion engines.

TWO-POWER STANDARD

In the last two decades of the nineteenth century, supremacy on the high seas unquestionably rested with Great Britain. New ideas and inventions were emerging so quickly that a new vessel could be obsolete before it was launched. Much of this problem was created by Britain's own naval policy, which was described as a 'two-power standard' and which

kept the Royal Navy equal in numbers to any two foreign navies. In simple terms, warships were being built at too fast a rate to incorporate the latest technological advances.

In 1889, the two-power standard was modified somewhat when the Naval Defence Act came into force, decreeing that the Royal Navy must be capable of matching the world's second and third largest navies. The result was a new phase of shipbuilding, and at its forefront was the 'Royal Sovereign' class of battleship. Apart from the *Royal Sovereign* herself, there were seven vessels in the class: the *Empress of India, Ramillies, Repulse, Resolution, Revenge, Royal Oak* and *Hood*. A highly successful design, the Royal Sovereigns were faster than any contemporary battleships. Their main armament of four 343mm (13.5in) guns was mounted in twin barbettes; they also carried 10 152mm (6in) guns, 16 6-pounder guns and seven 45.7cm (18in) torpedo tubes. The exception was the *Hood*, whose main armament was mounted in turrets. The barbette arrangement, which saved a great deal of weight, meant that the Royal Sovereigns were a deck higher than contemporary low-freeboard battleships, and except for the *Hood* were far better seaboats. They displaced 14,377 tonnes (14,150 tons), carried a complement of 712, had a maximum speed of 30km/h (16.5kt) and an endurance of 8746km (4720nm).

In the 1890s the Royal Navy, closely followed by other major naval powers, developed a new standard type of battleship later known the the 'pre-dreadnought'. The first was 12,548-tonne (12,350-ton) *Renown* of 1892, but it was the 'Majestic' class of 1893–94 that served as the pattern for battleship design for the next decade. Displacing 15,129 tonnes (14,890 tons) they were armed with four 305mm (12in) guns, 12 152mm (6in) guns, 16 76mm (12-pdr) guns and 12 47mm (3-pdr) guns, as well as five 457mm (18in) torpedo tubes. In all, 42 pre-dreadnoughts were built for the Royal Navy up to 1904.

ARMOURED CRUISER

The late nineteenth century also saw the adoption by the Royal Navy of the armoured cruiser, the first of which were the 'Cressy' and 'Drake' classes of 1898. They were armed with two 234mm (9.2in) and 12 152mm (6in) guns and had an armoured belt on the waterline. Capable of 40km/h (22kt), they carried a complement of 760–900. Thirty-four were built up to 1904, the other classes being 'Monmouth' (10 ships), 'Devonshire' (six), 'Duke of Edinburgh' (two), 'Warrior' (four), and 'Minotaur' (three).

It was not these large warships that brought about the real revolution in naval affairs in the nineteenth century, however, but a much smaller instrument of war – the torpedo. All the major navies had adopted the self-propelled torpedo by the 1880s, the latest models having a range of about 500m (1640ft) at a speed of 18 knots, and the original compressed air method of propulsion was gradually giving way

to electric motors. Capital ships and specially designed torpedo boats – the first of which was the 25m (84ft) HMS *Lightning*, capable of 20 knots – both deployed torpedoes from tubes or launch cradles. Because torpedoes had to be launched from close range, torpedo boats were extremely vulnerable to defensive fire, but an exercise conducted by the Royal Navy in 1885 showed that although all the attacking craft were 'sunk', some of their practice torpedoes got through. The solution was to counter the torpedo boats with gun-armed 'catchers' that could be deployed from capital ships, and by the 1890s these had evolved into larger, independent vessels called 'torpedo boat destroyers' designed to accompany larger units. In 1892–93, the first six ships, now called simply 'destroyers', were ordered for service with the Royal Navy.

By 1895, 36 destroyers, led by HMS *Gossamer* and HMS *Rattlesnake*, had been launched. They were capable of 27

LEFT: HMS Benbow, launched in 1885, was an 'Admiral' class battleship, the others being the Camperdown, Howe and Rodney. She spent her whole career in the Mediterranean.

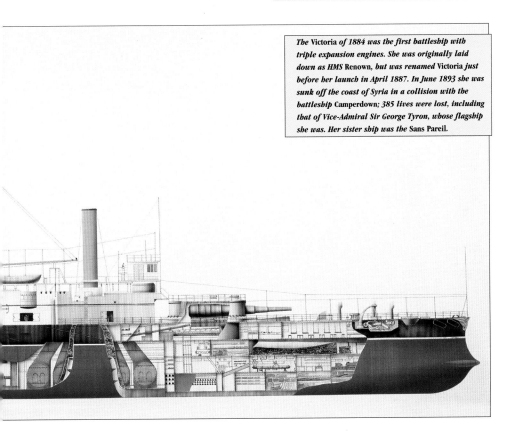

The Victoria *of 1884 was the first battleship with triple expansion engines. She was originally laid down as HMS* Renown, *but was renamed* Victoria *just before her launch in April 1887. In June 1893 she was sunk off the coast of Syria in a collision with the battleship* Camperdown; *385 lives were lost, including that of Vice-Admiral Sir George Tyron, whose flagship she was. Her sister ship was the* Sans Pareil.

knots, but the torpedo boats then being built could reach 24, so the speed margin was slender. They were succeeded by an improved class, the first of which were HMS *Havoc* and HMS *Hornet*, which could make in excess of 30 knots and which were armed with two torpedo tubes mounted on the centreline, one 12-pounder and five 6-pounder guns. Sixty-eight were built, their displacement gradually increasing from 285 to 365 tonnes (280 to 360 tons).

However, torpedo boats and destroyers were not to retain their pre-eminence as torpedo carriers. By the turn of the century, the British Admiralty, which had hitherto shown a complete lack of interest in submarines (a despicable, 'un-English' weapon of war) could no longer afford to ignore the fact that the French and Americans already possessed them in small numbers. The 1901–02 Naval Estimates made provision for the building of five improved boats of the 'Holland' type (an American design) for evaluation. The first five boats to be commissioned were built under licence by Vickers at Barrow-in-Furness.

The company and the Navy's newly appointed Inspecting-Captain of Submarines, Captain Reginald Bacon, set about making a series of improvements, so that when HM Submarine *No 1* was launched on 2 November 1902, she bore little resemblance to her American progenitor. Displacing 105 tonnes (104 tons) on the surface and 124 tonnes (122 tons) submerged, she was 19.3m (63ft 4in) long and had a maximum beam of 3.6m (11ft 9in). Her four-cylinder petrol engine developed 160hp, giving a maximum surface speed of about eight knots. Submerged, driven by an electric motor driven by a six-cell battery, she could make a maximum five knots. Her armament comprised a single 35.5cm (14in) torpedo tube and she carried a crew of seven.

In March 1904, all five boats of the 'A' class, as they were now called, took part in a simulated attack on the cruiser *Juno* off Portsmouth. It was successful, but *A1* was involved in a collision with a passenger liner and sank with all hands. In all, 13 'A' class boats were built, with 11 'B' class and 38 'C' class. From now on, the submarine was to be one of the Royal Navy's principal weapons of war, and its development would not be allowed to stagnate. For the submarine now had a powerful advocate, appointed First Sea Lord on Trafalgar Day, 1904. His name was Admiral Sir John Fisher.

CHAPTER 3

DREADNOUGHTS

The appearance of the *Dreadnought* in 1906 changed the face of naval warfare. Before that, Britain had built warships in large numbers to maintain the so-called 'two-power standard'. The *Dreadnought* began an arms race with Germany in the years leading up to World War I.

'Jackie' Fisher, as he was known throughout the Service, was a comparative rarity in Queen Victoria's navy: a senior officer with a firm grasp of scientific and technological principles. An exponent of gunnery, he harboured a long-standing ambition to improve the fleet's standard of shooting, and during his time in command of the British Mediterranean Fleet he had demonstrated that engagements were feasible at

ABOVE: The development of the battlecruiser proceeded in parallel with that of the dreadnought. Pictured here is HMS Inflexible. Her sister ships were Indomitable and Invincible.

LEFT: HMS Neptune of 1909 had a new turret arrangement to provide greater broadside fire, with amidships turrets in echelon and 'X' turret superfiring over 'Y' turret, as clearly seen here.

ranges of 5484m (6000yds) and that modern guns could achieve a good hit rate at up to 7312m (8000yds), provided they were deliberately aimed and that full salvoes were fired. It followed that the chances of success in a long-range naval duel would rise in direct proportion to the number of large-calibre guns that could be brought into action.

By the time he took over as First Sea Lord at the age of 58, Fisher had already put a lot of thought into the concept of a battleship armed with a maximum number of 254mm (10in) guns at the expense of secondary armament, and within weeks of his appointment in 1904 he appointed a committee to design a battleship armed with the maximum number of 305mm (12in) guns, this calibre being preferred by the Admiralty. The committee was also to study the concept of a second type of warship, which would carry a battery of

ABOVE: *The first of her kind: HMS* Dreadnought *was the first battleship to feature a main armament of a single calibre (10 305mm/12in guns). She served with the Grand Fleet until 1916.*

305mm (12in) guns but which would have a speed of 45km/h (25kt) or thereabouts. This vessel would be in the nature of a hybrid, a cross between a heavy cruiser and a battleship – in other words, a 'battlecruiser'.

The 'super-battleship' concept took shape rapidly, its development spurred on by the acceleration of the international naval arms race, and a prototype was laid down by Portsmouth Dockyard in October 1905. It was constructed in great secrecy and in record time, the vessel being ready for initial sea trials a year and a day later. The name given to the formidable new ship was *Dreadnought*.

The *Dreadnought* was revolutionary in that she was armed with 10 30cm (12in) guns, two in each of five turrets centrally placed on the ship. (In fact, only eight guns in the first of these ships could be fully brought to bear, but this was remedied in its successors.) From 1906 onwards, a first-class battleship was to be a ship capable of firing 10 heavy guns on either side. Thus a dreadnought could engage one of the older vessels with a superiority of 10n to four, or two of them with a superiority of 10 to eight. As well as being the first battleship with main armament of a single calibre, *Dreadnought* was also the first with steam turbines and quadruple screws, machinery that gave her a top speed of 38km/h (21kt). She carried a crew of 697 and displaced 18,187 tonnes (17,900 tons).

Once the concept of the dreadnought had been proven, construction of this revolutionary type of battleship proceeded rapidly, at the rate of three or four per year. The original *Dreadnought* was followed by the *Bellerophon*, *Superb* and *Temeraire*, all laid down in 1906; the *Collingwood*, *St Vincent* and *Vanguard*, 1907; *Colossus*, *Hercules* and *Neptune*, 1908; *Conqueror*, *Monarch*, *Orion* and *Thunderer*, 1909; *Ajax*, *Audacious*, *Centurion* and *King George V*, 1910; *Benbow*, *Emperor of India*, *Iron Duke* and *Marlborough*, 1911; *Barham*, *Malaya*, *Queen Elizabeth*, *Valiant* and *Warspite*, 1912; and *Ramillies*, *Resolution*, *Revenge*, *Royal Oak* and *Royal Sovereign*, 1913. The 'Queen Elizabeth' class ships of 1912 were designed as fast battleships to replace battlecruisers as the offensive wing of the battle fleet, their task to engage enemy battleships. They were the first battleships to have 381mm (15in) guns and oil-fired engines.

Fisher's critics claimed that his introduction of the dreadnought made the great mass of British battleships obsolete and vulnerable, but those who supported him had come to realize that secondary armament was now of minor importance. The increasing range of torpedoes was making close-in actions dangerous; if a battleship could engage its adversary at really long range, its 152mm (6in) and 230mm (9in) secondary guns were irrelevant. Gunnery experts realized that at the immense ranges now possible for 305mm (12in) guns – 12,810m (14,000yds) or more – only the biggest guns would count. Effective ranging depended on the firing of salvoes, and having a greater number of shells in the salvo. A full salvo from a dreadnought meant that 3.85 tonnes (3.79 tons) of high explosive was on its way to the enemy over 15km (8nm) away.

NEW CLASS

The other revolutionary warship concept, the battlecruiser, was a vessel nearly equal in armament to the new battleships but very much swifter, a ship that could cruise ahead and scout for the main battle fleet, and be capable of overwhelming any conventional cruiser. In fact, the concept arose from the simple fact that existing armoured cruisers had evolved into ships so large and expensive that they had reached the end of their development potential.

The first ship of the new class was the *Inflexible*, completed in 1908. She carried eight 305mm (12in) guns and had a speed of 47km/h (26kt). Her firepower was four-fifths that of a dreadnought, but a lot had to be sacrificed in the cause of speed. While the indicated horsepower of the *Dreadnought* was 18,000, that of the *Inflexible* was 41,000, so a large hull was needed to accommodate the necessary 31 boilers. With a reduced armament, and protection sacrificed for speed, the battlecruisers were inevitably more vulnerable, as events at Jutland in 1916 were to show in a tragic manner.

Inflexible's sister ships were the *Indomitable* and *Invincible*; all displaced 17,527 tonnes (17,250 tons) and carried a complement of 784. They were followed by the *Australia*, *Indefatigable* and *New Zealand*, laid down in 1908–09; *Lion*, *Princess Royal* and

LEFT: Admiral Sir John Fisher, known as 'Jackie' to all ranks in the Royal Navy, revolutionized Britain's fleet. He was also a difficult man to deal with and upset many of his subordinates.

Queen Mary (1909–10); *Tiger* (1911); *Renown* and *Repulse* (1914); and *Hood* (1915). Although classed as a battlecruiser, *Hood* was in fact an enlarged 'Queen Elizabeth' type dreadnought, designed to counter the formidable German 'Mackensen' class battlecruisers laid down at the beginning of 1915. Displacing 41,861 tonnes (41,200 tons), she was the largest warship in the world when completed, and was to remain so until World War II.

Three other ships in this class, *Anson*, *Howe* and *Rodney*, were also laid down during World War I, but subsequently cancelled; their names were later allocated to a new generation of battleship. In the years before the outbreak of World War I, the mighty dreadnoughts and battlecruisers were visible manifestations of Britain's overwhelming seapower. Yet behind the scenes, virtually unnoticed, events had been unfolding which would make all of them obsolete within the next half-century.

On 4 May 1912, Commander C.R. Samson, a pilot with the newly formed Naval Wing of the Royal Flying Corps – later to become the Royal Naval Air Service – provided one of the highlights of the Fleet Review at Weymouth by flying a Short S27 biplane from the foredeck of the pre-dreadnought battleship HMS *Hibernia* as she steamed into wind at 18km/h (10kt).

HMS Dreadnought served with the Grand Fleet throughout her career. On 18 March 1915 she rammed and sank the German submarine U29 in the North Sea. After being withdrawn from the Grand Fleet, she served as a guardship in the Thames Estuary, 1916–1918. On 9 May 1921 she was sold and later broken up at Inverkeithing, Scotland.

LEFT: HMS Indomitable, *a battlecruiser of the 'Invincible' class. She fought in the Battle of the Dogger Bank and at Jutland, and also saw service in the Dardanelles. She was sold and broken up at Dover in 1921.*

It was the first time that a British aircraft had taken off from a moving ship.

A year later, the old cruiser HMS *Hermes* was commissioned as the headquarters ship of the Naval Wing. She was fitted with a trackway on her forecastle, from which an 80hp Caudron amphibian made several trials flights during the summer of 1913, and was later equipped with three Short S41 floatplanes. In July 1913, for the first time, aircraft were used by the Royal Navy in conjunction with surface vessels during a series of fleet manoeuvres, and aircraft from the *Hermes* carried out important experiments in wireless telegraphy.

In the summer of 1913, the Admiralty purchased a second seaplane tender. A 7518-tonne (7400-ton) merchant vessel then under construction at Blyth, Northumberland, she was

BELOW: The 'Dreadnought' class battleship HMS Warspite *had a long career that took her from Jutland in 1916 to Salerno in 1943. She was badly damaged in both actions, in the latter by bombs.*

commissioned in 1914 and honoured with a very famous name: *Ark Royal*. Three more seaplane tenders, the *Empress*, *Engadine* and *Riviera* – all cross-Channel packets – were requisitioned and converted in the summer of 1914. No one could have envisaged, then, that naval aviation would one day become a potent striking force that would decide the outcome of battles, and hound mighty capital ships to their destruction. As the war clouds gathered in 1914, it was the submarine that was seen, rightly, as the principal threat to dominion of the seas.

The Royal Navy's submarine fleet had come a long way in the decade since Admiral Fisher's appointment as First Sea Lord. One of his first acts had been to launch a massive submarine construction programme; he had demanded 'more submarines at once – at least 25 in addition to those now building and ordered, and 100 more as soon as practical'.

By 1910, the Royal Navy's submarine flotillas had a total of 12 A-class boats, 11 Bs, and 37 Cs. Built by Vickers, all were progressive improvements of the original Holland design. The 'C' class had a length of 43.4m (142.3ft) and displaced 292 tonnes (287 tons) surfaced. A new class, the 'D', was also laid down; designed for overseas service, the 'D' boats were 50.2m (164ft 7in) long and displaced 503 tonnes (495 tons) on the surface, 629 tonnes (620 tons) submerged. They were the first British twin-screw submarines and, for surface-running, petrol engines were abandoned in favour of heavy oil (diesel) engines. Although beset by teething problems, they were far safer than petrol engines and gave off fewer noxious

THE FATE OF THE DREADNOUGHTS

The table below gives brief details of the service and fate of the 21 'Dreadnought' class battleships built up to 1912.

Dreadnought (1905). Grand Fleet 1914–15. Rammed and sank *U29* in North Sea, 18 March 1915. Broken up 1921.

Bellerophon (1906). Damaged in two collisions, 1911 and 1914. Grand Fleet, 1914–18. Jutland, 1916. Broken up 1921.

Superb (1907). Grand Fleet, 1914–18. Jutland, 1916. Gunnery target ship, 1920. Broken up 1921.

Temeraire (1907). Grand Fleet, 1914–18. Jutland, 1916. Mediterranean, 1918. Cadet training ship, 1919. Broken up 1921.

Collingwood (1908). Grand Fleet, 1914–18. Jutland, 1916. Gunnery training ship, 1919. Broken up 1922.

St Vincent (1907). Grand Fleet, 1914–18. Jutland, 1916. Broken up 1921.

Vanguard (1908). Originally laid down as *Rodney*. Grand Fleet 1914–17. Jutland 1916. Destroyed by explosion at Scapa Flow, 9 July 1917 (804 dead).

Colossus (1909). Grand Fleet, 1914–18. Jutland, 1916 (hit twice). Cadet training ship, 1919. Broken up 1922.

Hercules (1909). Damaged in collision, 1913. Grand Fleet, 1914–18. Jutland, 1916. Broken up 1921.

Neptune (1909). Originally laid down as *Foudroyant*. Grand Fleet, 1914–18. Jutland, 1916. Damaged in collision, April 1916. Broken up 1922.

Conqueror (1910). Grand Fleet, 1914–18. Jutland, 1916. Damaged in collision with battleship *Monarch*, December 1914. Broken up 1922.

Monarch (1910). Grand Fleet, 1914–18. Jutland, 1916. Badly damaged in collision with *Conqueror*, December 1914. Target ship, 1922. Sunk as target by battleship *Revenge* off Scilly Islands, January 1925.

Orion (1909). Damaged in collision with battleship *Revenge*, January 1912. Grand Fleet, 1914–18. Jutland, 1916. Broken up 1922.

Thunderer (1910). Grand Fleet, 1914–18. Jutland, 1916. Cadet training ship, 1922. Ran aground en route to breaker's yard at Blyth, 1924.

Ajax (1911). Grand Fleet, 1914–18. Jutland, 1916. Mediterranean and Black Sea, 1919–24. Broken up 1926.

Audacious (1911). Sunk by mine off Tory Island, Donegal, 27 October 1914 (crew safe).

Centurion (1911). Collided with and sank Italian steamer *Derna*, 9 December 1912. Grand Fleet, 1914–18. Jutland, 1916. Mediterranean and Black Sea, 1919–24. Target ship, 1926. Converted to dummy battleship, 1941 (representing HMS *Anson*). Floating AA battery, Suez, 1944. Sunk off Normandy, 9 June 1944, as part of artificial harbour.

King George V (1911). Originally laid down as *Royal George*. Grand Fleet, 1914–18. Jutland, 1916. Mediterranean, 1919–23. Gunnery training ship, 1923–26. Broken up 1926.

Benbow (1912). Grand Fleet, 1914–18. Jutland, 1916. Mediterranean and Black Sea, 1919–26. Broken up 1931.

Emperor of India (1912). Originally laid down as *Delhi*. Grand Fleet, 1914–18. Mediterranean, 1919–26. Refit, 1922. Sunk as target, 1931, refloated and broken up.

Iron Duke (1912). Grand Fleet, 1914–18. Jutland, 1916. Mediterranean and Black Sea, 1919–26. Gunnery training ship, 1931. Damaged in air attack, Scapa Flow, October 1939. Broken up 1946.

Marlborough (1912). Grand Fleet, 1914–18. Severely damaged by German torpedo attack, Jutland, 1916. Mediterranean and Black Sea, 1919–26. Refit, 1920–22. Broken up 1932.

---

fumes. During exercises in 1910, the crew of the prototype submarine *D1* proved a point when, despite trouble with one engine, they took their boat from Portsmouth to the west coast of Scotland and remained on station off an 'enemy' anchorage for three days, claimingsuccessful dummy torpedo attacks on two cruisers.

The 'E' class, a straightforward development of the 'D', was just beginning to enter service at the outbreak of World War I. Displacing 677 tonnes (667 tons) surfaced, 820 tonnes (807 tons) submerged, the 'E' class boats carried a crew of 30 and were armed with five torpedo tubes, two in the bow, one in the stern and two amidships. This arrangement meant that the boat had to turn through no more than 45 degrees to engage any target. In all, 55 'E' class submarines were built between 1913 and 1916. They were to become the mainstay of the Royal Navy's submarine fleet in World War I, operating in every theatre of war, and their exploits were to become legendary. A quarter of a century later, though, it would be submarines of another country which would grab the glory at the Royal Navy's expense.

CHAPTER 4

WORLD WAR I

On the outbreak of World War I, Britain had 20 Dreadnoughts with 12 more under construction, compared to Germany's 15 and six. Battlecruisers numbered nine to Germany's five. Scapa Flow in the Orkneys was the only base large enough to accommodate the Grand Fleet.

Although the hostilities of World War I were eventually to encompass virtually the whole world, the naval war was decided by the fleets of two nations: Britain and Germany. From the outset, the task facing the Royal Navy was prodigious. Not only had it to protect the shores of Britain from the threat of invasion; it also had to protect the maritime convoys that were vital to the country's survival, and to secure the

ABOVE: From the beginnings of World War I, new-built British battleships and battlecruisers had a standard main armament of 381mm (15in) guns, the former with eight and the latter four.

LEFT: A battleship of the 1913 'Royal Sovereign' class, HMS Revenge, seen here firing a broadside, was converted from coal to mixed fuel during the course of construction.

Channel area so that there was no interference with the constant flow of supplies and personnel to the Western Front.

Above all, the Germans, whose fleet was greatly outnumbered, feared a major attack on their principal naval base of Wilhelmshaven by the British Grand Fleet, based as Scapa Flow in the Orkneys. They would soon left in no doubt that the Royal Navy intended to follow an aggressive policy. On 28 August 1914, a force of British warships from Harwich, commanded by Commodore Tyrwhitt, swept into the Heligoland Bight and took the enemy completely by surprise. Destroyers of the 1st and 3rd Flotillas, led by the cruisers *Arethusa* and *Fearless*, engaged in a furious battle with German destroyers and cruisers. The *Arethusa* was disabled in the action, but the German cruiser *Mainz* and the destroyer leader *V187* were sunk. Later, five British battlecruisers under

Admiral Sir David Beatty came up in support, sinking the German cruisers *Köln* and *Ariadne*. Two other German light cruisers and three destroyers were damaged.

Any elation at this British victory soon dissipated with news of a British defeat in the South Atlantic a few weeks later. On the outbreak of war, a German naval squadron under Vice-Admiral Graf von Spee, which had been deployed to Tsingtao in China, set out on the long voyage home. It comprised the armoured cruisers *Scharnhorst* and *Gneisenau* and three light cruisers (*Leipzig, Dresden* and *Nürnberg*) and by the end of October 1914 it was off the west coast of South America, ready to round Cape Horn and enter the Atlantic. All that stood between it was a scratch British naval squadron under Admiral Sir Christopher Cradock,

comprising the armoured cruisers *Good Hope* and *Monmouth*, a light cruiser, the *Glasgow*, the auxiliary vessel *Otranto* and the old pre-dreadnought battleship *Canopus*.

The 14,224-tonne (14,000-ton) *Good Hope*, completed in 1912, carried one old 23.3cm (9.2in) gun forward and another aft, as well as 16 15.2cm (6in) guns of an equally old pattern; the 9957-tonne (9800-ton) *Monmouth*, completed in 1913, had a main armament of 14 15.2cm (6in) guns, also of an obsolete pattern. The *Glasgow*, launched in 1909, had two 15.2cm (6in) and 10 10cm (4in) guns of a newer type. The auxiliary vessel, the *Otranto*, was a converted liner of the Orient company, and in no sense did she count as a fighting unit. The old *Canopus*, dating from 1897, had four 30.4cm (12in) guns, but her best speed was barely 15 knots, which was hardly adequate against adversaries that could make 22. In the event, she took no part in the coming action, and was 463km (250nm) away when, on 1 November 1914, *Good Hope, Monmouth, Glasgow* and *Otranto* sighted Admiral von

Spee's squadron off Coronel, on the coast of Chile. Hopelessly outgunned and outranged, *Good Hope* and *Monmouth* were soon on fire, and in the evening *Good Hope* exploded and sank. *Monmouth* went down soon afterwards, whereupon *Glasgow* broke off her own attack and steamed away to join *Canopus*. Both ships headed for the Falkland Islands, where they were ordered to defend the wireless station, coal and oil stores.

CAPE HORN

The destruction of Admiral Cradock's squadron created a dangerous situation in the South Atlantic. Von Spee was now in a position to paralyse South American shipping; he might even cross the Atlantic to attack the South African mercantile routes. Oddly enough, he failed to exploit this golden opportunity. Instead, after his ships had been replenished and his crews rested off Chile, he planned to attack the Falklands and seize the facilities there. In London, Admiral Sir John Fisher anticipated von Spee's plan and dispatched his Chief of Staff, Vice-Admiral Sir Frederick Doveton Sturdee, southwards with the battlecruisers *Invincible* and *Inflexible*. At the same time, orders were issued to the British warships on station off the Central and Southern American coasts – the cruisers *Cornwall*, *Kent*, *Caernarvon* and *Bristol* – to make for the Falklands with all speed and join the *Glasgow* and *Canopus* there.

Von Spee's squadron rounded Cape Horn early in December, and on 8 December sighted the Falklands. As the five German warships steamed towards the wireless station they came under fire from the *Canopus*, and just as they were preparing to fire their own first salvoes, three British cruisers

*BELOW: **The dreadnought** Queen Elizabeth **pictured just after completion in 1915. She saw service in the Dardanelles and was subsequently to see extensive service in World War II.***

LEFT: The crew of a 15cm (6in) gun battery passing ammunition through an anti-flash screen around 1917. Flashbacks from the armament were the cause of several serious accidents.

help beat off any possible torpedo attacks by the British light cruisers. At about 0920 hours, von Spee drew his ships up in a new battle-line 16km (10 miles) from the harbour. It was headed by the *Gneisenau*, with the *Dresden* next, then the *Scharnhorst*, *Nürnberg* and *Leipzig*. What the Germans were seeking was a running battle in which they would easily be able to out-manoeuvre their opponents.

What von Spee did not know was that, hidden behind the heights surrounding the harbour, were the British battlecruisers *Invincible* and *Inflexible*. They had arrived only the day before and had been busily fuelling. Now, at 0945, they emerged under cover of a smokescreen laid by the last British cruiser to leave the anchorage. Too late,

were sighted coming out of the bay on East Falkland. Von Spee continued to manoeuvre his two principal ships into a position where they could concentrate their heavy guns on *Canopus*, and also ordered the *Leipzig* to come into action and

Launched in October 1913, the dreadnought Queen Elizabeth *underwent two major reconstructions between the world wars and saw service in the Mediterranean in World War II. Severely damaged in Alexandria harbour by Italian frogmen, she was repaired in America and went on to serve in the Indian Ocean with the Eastern Fleet.*

Admiral von Spee realised that he and his ships had fallen into a carefully laid trap.

At 1230 hours, Admiral Sturdee increased the speed of his two battlecruisers to 50km/h (28kt) and, leaving the *Caernarvon*, *Kent* and *Cornwall* behind, closed and opened fire on the rearmost German vessel from a range of 15,700m (17,000yds). Von Spee, realising that he could not out-run the British, turned broadside on and engaged the *Invincible*, while the *Gneisenau* took on the *Inflexible*. The three German light cruisers fell out of the battle-line and scattered for the nearest neutral port, pursued by the *Kent*, *Cornwall* and *Glasgow*, while the *Caernarvon* followed the battlecruisers to lend assistance if necessary.

FLEEING ENEMY

Sturdee used the same tactics against von Spee that the latter had used against Admiral Cradock, using his superior speed and gunnery to good effect. At 1617 hours, after a running fight of some three hours, the *Scharnhorst* went down by the stern and the two British battlecruisers turned their joint fire on the *Gneisenau*, which continued to fight on very gallantly, battered into a blazing wreck, until she too sank at about 1800. About 200 survivors were rescued from her 800-strong crew; all 860 men aboard the *Scharnhorst* perished

The British cruisers, meanwhile, had caught up with the fleeing enemy ships. In the ensuing battle, the *Leipzig* was sunk by *Glasgow* and *Cornwall*, while *Nürnberg* was sunk by HMS *Kent* after a five-hour pursuit. Captain Allen of the *Kent* had exhorted his engineers and stokers to achieve the impossible as the *Kent* was sister ship to the *Monmouth*, which the *Nürnberg* had sunk and left her survivors to drown. The men of the *Kent* were eager for revenge, and they achieved it by feeding their ship's fires with anything that would burn. For a time they actually pushed the old cruiser to go a knot or two faster than she had ever done in the days of her prime, until their efforts brought her guns within range of the enemy.

Of von Spee's Pacific Squadron, only the *Dresden* escaped. But her days were numbered, too. On 14 March 1915, the cruisers *Kent* and *Glasgow* caught up with her off Juan Fernandez and she was scuttled by her crew after receiving crippling damage.

The news of Sturdee's victory off the Falklands was soon tempered by the shock and horror of an event that occurred only a week later. The Germans, hoping to lure part of the British Fleet into an ambush, decided to carry out a series of hit-and-run attacks on British east coast towns. The British Admiralty was aware of these plans, because its experts had broken the German naval codes, but it nevertheless came as a

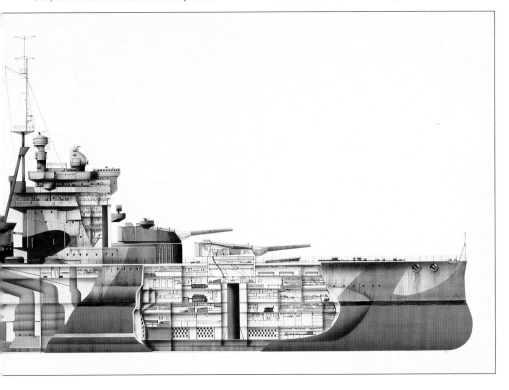

shock when, in the early morning of 16 December 1914, the German battlecruisers *Seydlitz, Moltke* and *Blücher* bombarded West Hartlepool, while the *Derfflinger* and von der Tann shelled Scarborough and Whitby, killing 127 civilians (including 78 women and children) and injuring 567. The *Moltke* and *Blücher* were hit by shore batteries, but all the raiders escaped in the mist.

British forces – the 1st Battlecruiser Squadron under Admiral Beatty and the 2nd Battle Squadron under Admiral Warrender – were already at sea to intercept the attackers, which were sighted on their approach to the coast by British destroyers. At 0445 hours, the latter were engaged by the German cruiser *Hamburg* and escorting light forces, which disabled the destroyer HMS *Hardy* and damaged *Ambuscade* and *Lynx*. During the forenoon the German battlecruisers, returning from their attack, passed some miles astern of the 2nd Battle Squadron, which sighted the German ships and turned to close with them – only to be thwarted by deteriorating weather and ambiguous signals from Beatty, which led to the light cruisers breaking off the chase. So a golden opportunity to inflict punishing damage on the enemy was lost.

Another opportunity was squandered on 24 January 1915, when the Germans set out on an offensive sweep of the southeastern Dogger Bank. Beatty's 1st Battlecruiser Squadron, comprising his flagship HMS *Lion*, together with

the *Princess Royal, Tiger, New Zealand* and *Invincible*, sighted the German battlecruisers *Seydlitz, Moltke* and *Derfflinger*, together with the armoured cruiser *Blücher*, six light cruisers and a number of destroyers, steering westward. The German warships turned and made for home, but were pursued at 50km/h (28kt) and brought to battle at 0900 east of the Dogger Bank. HMS *Lion* led the British line, but dropped out after she was hit, Beatty transferring his flag to the *Princess Royal*. During the action the *Blücher* was sunk and the *Derfflinger* and *Seydlitz* seriously damaged. Much more damage might have been inflicted on the Germans had not Beatty, thinking he had spotted a submarine's periscope, ordered his ships to alter course, enabling the enemy to escape.

It was not until 31 May 1916 that the British and German Main Battle Fleets came face to face, at Jutland. The battle that followed was complex, and is best described in the terse words of the Battle Summary that gives a minute-by-minute account of the action. The British forces comprised the Battlecruiser Fleet (1st and 2nd Squadrons), with HMS *Lion* (Admiral Beatty), *Princess Royal* (Admiral Brock), *Tiger, Queen Mary, New Zealand* (Admiral Pakenham) and *Indefatigable*, supported by the 5th Battle Squadron with HMS *Barham* (Admiral Evan-Thomas), *Warspite, Valiant* and *Malaya*, in advance of the Main Battle Fleet, the latter under the command of Admiral Lord Jellicoe.

2.20 p.m. British Light Forces ahead of Battlecruiser Fleet sighted German ships to ESE. Admiral Beatty turned SSE, course for Horn Reef, to intercept.

2.35 p.m. Admiral Beatty altered to E and NE towards

heavy smoke visible ENE. Seaplane carrier *Engadine* sent up seaplane scout; first such reconnaissance in action.

3.31 p.m. Admiral Beatty sighted German Battlecruiser Squadron – HIMSS (His Imperial Majesty's Ships) *Lützow* (Admiral Hipper), *Derfflinger*, *Seydlitz*, *Moltke* and *Von der Tann* – steering ENE. Battlecruiser Fleet, on line of bearing, closed German squadron from 23,000 yards on ESE course at 25 knots; 5th Battle Squadron, 10,000 yards astern, conformed.

3.48 p.m. Both battlecruiser forces opened fire almost simultaneously at about 18,500 yards. Action on ESE to SSE course.

4.00 p.m. Range about 16,000 yards.

4.06 p.m. Indefatigable hit by salvo from *Von der Tann*; magazine exploded; ship sunk by another salvo.

4.08 p.m. British 5th Battle Squadron in action at 19,000–20,000 yards; German Light Cruiser Squadron driven off to eastwards.

4.15 p.m. Destroyer action: two German TBDs sunk; *Nestor* and *Nomad* disabled; sunk later by German Battle Fleet.

4.26 p.m. *Queen Mary* hit by salvo from *Derfflinger*; magazine exploded; ship sunk.

4.42 p.m. Admiral Beatty sighted German High Seas Fleet under Admiral Scheer (flagship *Friedrich der Grosse*) led by 3rd Squadron, steering northwards. British ships in succession turned 16 points to starboard; German battlecruisers followed suit, taking station ahead by High Seas Fleet. A time of this turn, Admiral Beatty and Admiral Jellicoe were over 50 miles apart and closing at about 45 miles per hour.

4.45 p.m. Battlecruiser action renewed on northerly course, with *Barham* and *Valiant* supporting Battlecruiser Fleet; *Warspite* and *Malaya* engaged at 19,000 yards German 1st and 3rd High Seas Squadrons.

5.00 p.m. British Battlecruiser Fleet outdistancing German ships on northerly run.

5.20 p.m. German battlecruisers ordered to give chase.

5.35 p.m. Admiral Beatty altered from NNE to NE to conform to signalled course of British Main Fleet.

5.42 p.m. British battlecruisers again in touch with German ships. *Lion* fired 15 salvoes during next 10 minutes.

6.00 p.m. Admiral Beatty sighted Main Fleet. Admiral Jellicoe (flagship *Iron Duke*) in Lat 57°11'N, Long 5°39'E, his main force having maintained since 4.00 p.m. a 'fleet speed' of 20 knots, on a course SE by S, with Battle Fleet in divisions line ahead disposed abeam to starboard.

6.02 p.m. Fleet speed reduced to 18 knots; subsequently reduced to 14 knots to allow battlecruisers to pass ahead.

6.16 p.m. Upon Admiral Beatty's report giving High Seas Fleet's position, Admiral Jellicoe signalled Battle Fleet to form line of battle on port wing column; course SE by E. At this point German battlecruisers sank the armoured cruiser *Defence* (Rear-Admiral Sir Robert Arbuthnot) and damaged *Warrior*, which shortly after 6.05 p.m. had crossed *Lion*'s bows from port to starboard in order to finish off *Wiesbaden*, one of the German light cruisers under their fire. Disabled *Warrior* passed astern of 5th Battle Squadron (turning to port to form astern of 6th Division) just as *Warspite*'s helm jammed; this mishap compelled the latter to continue her turn and brought her under heavy fire, but enabled *Warrior* to draw

BELOW: The 'Iron Duke' class dreadnought HMS Marlborough *was severely damaged when torpedoed by a German cruiser at Jutland in May 1916. She later served in the Mediterranean.*

LEFT: Admiral Sir David Beatty, commanding the Battlecruiser Fleet, pictured aboard his flagship HMS Lion. His battlecruisers sacrificed armour for speed and suffered for it at Jutland.

he able to transfer his flag to *Moltke*. Meanwhile *Derfflinger* led German battlecruisers.

6.54 p.m. *Marlborough* torpedoed, but continued in action.

7.00 p.m. Admiral Jellicoe ordered 2nd Battle Squadron to take station ahead of *Iron Duke;* 1st Battle Squadron to form astern. During the next half-hour, the British ships held their targets under intermittent but effective fire at ranges varying from 15,000 yards in the van to 8500 yards in the rear. German Fleet turning westward.

7.05 p.m. British line, after closing three points to starboard, turned away to avoid torpedo attack. German TBD *V48* sunk by gunfire.

7.15 p.m. Admiral Scheer, drawing off his main force, ordered his already battered battlecruisers to 'close the enemy'.

7.25 p.m. Another German torpedo attack successfully dealt with by British light forces.

7.33 p.m. British Fleet back on S by W course.

7.37 p.m. German battlecruisers broke off action: *Derfflinger* on fire.

7.40 p.m. Admiral Beatty reported German position to westward.

7.41 p.m. German Fleet no longer in sight from *Iron Duke;*

clear. In fact, the *Defence* was sunk by the battleship *Friedrich der Grosse*, with the loss of 893 lives – author.

Hereabouts, the 3rd Battlecruiser Squadron – *Invincible* (Admiral Hood) *Inflexible* and *Indomitable* – (detached by Admiral Jellicoe at 4.00 p.m. in support of Admiral Beatty), came up from the eastward, where with *Canterbury* and *Chester* it had engaged the German light cruiser screen in a sharp encounter in which the TBD *Shark* was sunk. Upon sighting *Lion*, Admiral Hood at 6.16 p.m. took station ahead of Battlecruiser Fleet and engaged German battlecruisers at 8600 yards. Soon after 6.30 p.m. *Invincible*, under repeated salvoes, notably from *Derfflinger*, blew up and sank; but Admiral Hood's arrival in commanding position on bow of German Fleet caused the latter to make large turn to starboard, his squadron being probably mistaken for the British Battle Fleet.

6.31 p.m. *Iron Duke* engaged leading ship of König Squadron at 12,000 yards; on the starboard wing *Marlborough* (Admiral Burney) had already opened fire at 6.17 p.m. on a ship of 'Kaiser' class at 13,000 yards.

6.33 p.m. Fleet speed increased to 17 knots. Action now joined, but impeded by mist and smoke. At the head of the German battlecruiser line *Lützow* hauled away badly damaged; *Derfflinger* ceased fire.

6.38 p.m. British deployment completed.

6.45 p.m. *Lion* once more leading Battlecruiser Fleet at head of British battle line in following formation: 1st Div. *King George V* (Admiral Jerram); 2nd Div. *Orion* (Admiral Leveson); 3rd Div.; *Iron Duke* (Admiral Jellicoe); 4th Div. *Benbow* (Admiral Sturdee); 5th Div. *Colossus* (Admiral Gaunt); 6th Div. *Marlborough* (Admiral Burney).

6.50 p.m. British Fleet altered course to S by divisions, to close German Fleet. Admiral Hipper left *Lützow*, which fell out on fire and with heavy list; not until about 9.00 p.m. was

RIGHT: The battlecruiser HMS Queen Mary explodes after being hit by a salvo from the German battlecruiser Derfflinger at Jutland. The death toll was 1266.

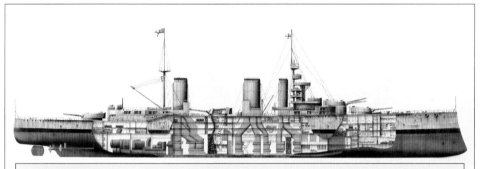

Admiral Beatty's flagship at Jutland, HMS Lion. In the previous year, she suffered 21 hits at the Battle of the Dogger Bank on 24 January 1915, and at Jutland she took a further 12 hits, narrowly escaping blowing up. She was sold and broken up at Blyth, Northumberland, in 1924.

British Battle Fleet altered course, by divisions, three points more to starboard (i.e. to the SW).

7.50 p.m. German TBD *S35* sunk by British 12th Flotilla.

7.59 p.m. British Fleet altered to W by divisions on sighting isolated German ships, which gradually turned away.

8.25 p.m. British Battlecruiser Fleet in effective touch with German ships for a few minutes.

8.30 p.m. British Fleet, after turn by divisions to SW, again in single line.

8.38 p.m. *Falmouth* last ship in touch with German Fleet.

NIGHT ACTION

9.00 p.m. British Fleet, after altering by divisions to S, formed divisions in line ahead disposed abeam to port, with columns one mile apart; destroyers five miles astern of Battle Fleet.

9.32 p.m. Minelaying flotilla leader *Abdiel* laid minefield 15 miles from Vyl Light.

10.04 p.m. British flotillas, after dropping astern, repelled attack by *Hamburg* and *Elbing*.

10.20 p.m. British 2nd Light Cruiser Squadron engaged ships of German 4 Scouting Group; German light cruiser *Frauenlob* sunk; British cruisers *Southampton* and *Dublin* damaged.

11.30 p.m. British 4th Flotilla engaged German cruisers; *Tipperary* sunk; *Broke* damaged and rammed *Sparrowhawk*, which was later abandoned. German light cruisers *Rostock* and *Elbing*, on port wing of 1st High Seas Squadron, at this period attempted to cross line to starboard, in order to escape torpedo attack; *Rostock* torpedoed; *Elbing* collided with battleship *Posen*; both cruisers later blown up.

Midnight – During this period remainder of 4th Flotilla twice engaged German battleships. *Fortune* and *Ardent* sunk; German battleship *Pommern* sunk, probably in this action. At this stage also, probably, British cruiser *Black Prince* sunk by

Thüringen and *Ostfriesland*, of 1st High Seas Squadron.

0.30 a.m. British TBD *Turbulent* rammed and sunk by German large vessel, which also damaged *Petard* by gunfire.

1.45 a.m. German battlecruiser *Lützow* now abandoned; crew taken off by German TBDs; ship sunk by torpedo.

2.00 a.m. British 12th Flotilla attacked German battleships at about 3000 yards. Disabled *Marlborough*, unable to maintain fleet speed, sent back to base under escort; Admiral Burney's flag transferred to *Revenge*.

2.35 a.m. British TBD *Moresby*, 13th Flotilla, attacked four Deutschland (class) battleships.

2.47 a.m. Dawn, 1 June 1916.

As daylight broke over the North Sea, the fleets dispersed, and by noon, both were returning to their respective bases. Jellicoe had intended to pursue the High Seas Fleet to its destruction; that he failed to do so was due to a combination of circumstances – vague reports, the failure of some of his captains to exercise initiative, the failure of the British Admiralty to relay certain vital intelligence on the movements of the enemy warships. And there was no escaping the fact that the Germans had meted out far more punishment than they had taken. They had lost one battleship, a battlecruiser, four cruisers and five destroyers, but the British had lost three battlecruisers, three cruisers and eight destroyers. British fatal casualties numbered 6097, against the German total of 2551.

Yet the Royal Navy had won a strategic victory. The next time the German High Seas Fleet left Wilhelmshaven in full strength would be in November 1918, after the German surrender, when it sailed into internment at Scapa Flow. There, in 1919, it would be scuttled by its own crews in a final act of defiance.

In the Mediterranean, the Royal Navy's principal area of operations was the Dardanelles. Turkey had come out on the side of the Central Powers (Germany and Austria) and her

THE ROYAL NAVY'S BALTIC WAR

In 1919, the Royal Navy found itself committed to a 'shooting war' in the Baltic and off North Russia, supporting the Allied Intervention Force which was in action against the Bolsheviks. First on the scene was the seaplane carrier *Pegasus*, which arrived off Murmansk with her Short floatplanes in the spring of 1919. Then, in July 1919, the new aircraft carrier *Vindictive* joined the naval force under Admiral Cowan that was operating in the Baltic off Kronstadt. She carried a mixed complement of Sopwith Camels, Short floatplanes and Sopwith Strutters, 12 aircraft in all, which she disembarked for land-based operations in the Gulf of Finland before returning to Copenhagen to collect more aircraft, which had been ferried from England by HMS *Argus*.

On 30 July 1919, *Vindictive*'s aircraft carried out two raids on Kronstadt. Another attack took place on 17 August, this time by night and with the object of diverting the attention of Bolshevik shore batteries from a raiding force of British MTBs. Altogether, *Vindictive*'s aircraft made some 60 raids on Kronstadt, and also acted as naval gunfire spotters.

In November 1919, a year after the Armistice on the Western Front, unrest among *Vindictive*'s crew flared into open mutiny as she replenished at Copenhagen. Sixteen men were subsequently tried and punished. A few days later, the *Vindictive* returned to the Gulf of Finland, re-embarked her aircraft and sailed for England with the rest of the Baltic Force at the end of December.

troops were pressing the Russians hard in the Caucasus. In an attempt to relieve the pressure, an Anglo-French combined operation was mounted, its aim to force a passage of the Dardanelles – the winding, treacherous 64km (40-mile) stretch of water leading from the Aegean to the Sea of Marmara – and land an expeditionary force before Constantinople (Istanbul), the belief being that such a show of strength would quickly force Turkey out of the war.

But the Turks were ready to confront such a plan. With German help they had mined the waters and installed powerful

shore batteries to cover the minefields, so that any attempt to sweep them would be met with devastating gunfire. Before the mines could be swept, the forts therefore had to be neutralised, and this could only be done by naval gunfire. A powerful Anglo-French naval force was assembled, comprising 14 pre-dreadnought battleships (four of them French), the battlecruiser *Inflexible* and the new dreadnought *Queen Elizabeth*.

MAXIMUM EFFORT

The bombardment of the forts at the entrance to the Dardanelles began on 19 February 1915, with aircraft from the seaplane carrier *Ark Royal* acting as spotters. The forts were shattered, enabling trawlers to sweep the first four miles of the straits, and on 26 February the pre-dreadnoughts *Albion*, *Majestic* and *Vengeance* proceeded to the limit of the swept area to bombard Fort Dardanus. The bombardments continued throughout March, other British ships involved including the pre-dreadnoughts *Triumph*, *Ocean*, *Canopus*, *Swiftsure*, *Cornwallis*, *Irresistible*, *Prince George*, *Agamemnon* and *Lord Nelson*, as well as the *Queen Elizabeth*, whose 38cm (15in) guns were powerful enough to hit the vulnerable reverse faces of the fortifications by shooting right across the peninsula with the help of spotting from the air.

Despite the weight of firepower, progress was slow and minelaying operations were thwarted by powerful searchlights and accurate enemy gunfire. In an attempt to break the deadlock, a maximum effort involving three squadrons of warships was mounted on 18 March 1915. It ended in disaster, the *Irresistible*, *Ocean* and the French *Bouvet* being mined and sunk, while *Inflexible* and the French *Gaulois* were damaged. The British losses were made good by the pre-dreadnoughts *Queen* and *Implacable*.

It was now becoming increasingly clear that without military support ashore, further attempts to force a passage of the Dardanelles would meet with failure, and consequently April 1915 saw the beginning of the disastrous Gallipoli campaign,

RIGHT: The second HMS Ark Royal. Originally constructed for as a merchant vessel, she was taken over by the Royal Navy for use as a seaplane carrier in 1913.

with Allied forces landing on the Gallipoli Peninsula in what was then the largest opposed amphibious invasion in history. Allied warships continued to support the ground forces until they were evacuated in January 1916, having suffered appalling attrition through enemy action and disease. The Royal Navy lost three more pre-dreadnoughts in the course of the campaign, the battleship *Goliath* being torpedoed by the Turkish destroyer *Muavenet* in May 1915 (570 dead) and the *Triumph* and *Majestic* being torpedoed by the German submarine *U21* in the same month (73 and 40 dead).

A GLIMPSE OF THE FUTURE

One Royal Navy vessel that made an everlasting name for herself in the Dardanelles campaign was the seaplane carrier *Ben-my-Chree*, which arrived on 12 June 1915. She carried two Short Seaplanes, recently converted to launch torpedoes, and these scored some successes against enemy transports. The *Ben-my-Chree* subsequently operated in the eastern Mediterranean, the Red Sea and the Indian Ocean during the latter part of 1916 and early 1917, until she was sunk by enemy gunfire off Castellorizo in Asia Minor in January of that year.

Yet the days of hybrid ships like the *Ben-my-Chree* were numbered. By 1917, the Royal Navy was a long way ahead of the rest of the world in the development of vessels that could truly be defined as aircraft carriers – in other words, fitted with flight decks from which aircraft were able to operate.

*ABOVE: **The seaplane carrier** Ben-my-Chree **operated in the Dardanelles, the eastern Mediterranean, the Red Sea and the Indian Ocean before being sunk by enemy gunfire in January 1917.***

The first such ship was the light battlecruiser HMS *Furious*, laid down shortly after the outbreak of war. Launched on 15 August 1916, she was fitted initially with a flight deck forward of her superstructure, but was eventually completed with a continuous flight deck and hangar accommodation for 16 aircraft (in 1918, Sopwith Camels). She was also fitted with workshops, electrically operated lifts from her hangar to the flight deck and a primitive form of arrester gear comprising strong rope nets suspended from crosspieces.

A similarly equipped vessel, HMS *Cavendish*, was commissioned in October 1918 and renamed HMS *Vindictive*, but her operational career was limited to a brief foray in support of the Allied Intervention Force in North Russia and the Baltic in 1919–20. The most important development was centred on three new carriers, all fitted with unbroken flight decks: the 11,024-tonne (10,850-ton) HMS *Hermes*, HMS *Argus* and HMS *Eagle*. Of the three, only HMS *Argus* joined the Fleet before the end of hostilities. Their day would come in a later war, when they, and others like them, would change the face of not only naval warfare, but of world power-projection forever, and would usher in a new phase of truly global war.

CHAPTER 5

THE BIGGEST NAVY IN THE WORLD

Between the world wars, a succession of treaties limited the tonnage and armament of new warships. Once the treaties were broken and war clouds loomed, naval yards worked to capacity to build new vessels and refit old ones.

At the end of the World War I the Royal Navy had 44 capital ships, plus one more in construction. By 1920 this total had been reduced to 29, a figure generally accepted as being the minimum number needed to defend Britain's worldwide interests and to maintain parity with the rapidly growing

ABOVE: The British Fleet lined up off Spithead, with the Royal Yacht carrying King George V moving between the ships. Naval reviews were always occasions of much pomp and ceremony.

LEFT: The battleship HMS Nelson at anchor in the Thames. The Nelson was a new vessel; launched in 1925 and completed in 1927, she served as flagship of the Home Fleet until 1941.

naval forces of the United States and Japan. But on 6 February 1922, the number of capital ships available to the Royal Navy was reduced still further with the signing of the Washington Naval Treaty.

The principal aim of the Washington Treaty, which was engineered by the United States and which in effect was the first disarmament treaty in history, was to limit the size of the navies of the five principal maritime powers, which at that time were Britain, the USA, France, Italy and Japan. For Britain, this meant a reduction in capital ship assets to 20 by scrapping existing warships and dropping new projects; however, because her capital ships were older and less heavily armed than those of the United States, she would be

ABOVE: *Launched in 1926, the cruiser HMS Kent went on to serve in the East Indies in 1939–40, and afterwards joined the Home Fleet. Placed in reserve in 1945, she was scrapped in 1948.*

permitted to build two new vessels as replacements for existing ones.

The other nations would also be permitted to build new capital ships to replace vessels that were 20 years old. This arrangement would allow France and Italy to lay down new warships in 1927, while Britain, the USA and Japan would not need to do so until 1931. No new capital ship was to exceed 35,562 tonnes (35,000 tons), nor mount guns larger than 40.5cm (16in). No existing capital ship was to be rebuilt, although an increase in deck armour against air attack was allowed, as were the addition of anti-torpedo bulges, provided these modifications did not exceed a total of 3048 tonnes (3000 tons).

NAVAL AVIATION

The Washington Treaty also limited the tonnage of current and planned aircraft carriers. Each signatory nation was allowed to build two vessels of up to 33,530 tonnes (33,000 tons); the remainder were limited to 27,433 tonnes (27,000 tons), and the total aircraft carrier tonnage in the case of Britain and the USA was not to exceed 137,167 tonnes (135,000 tons). Japan was allowed 82,300 tonnes (81,000 tons), while France and Italy were permitted 60,963 tonnes (60,000 tons) each. None of the carriers was allowed an armament in excess of eight 20cm (8in) guns, nor might they be replaced until they were 20 years old. No other warships were to be built in excess of 10,160 tonnes (10,000 tons), nor have guns larger than 20cm (8in).

Naval aviation, in which the Royal Navy had established a commanding lead by the end of World War I, had stagnated in the years since. By 1930, because of the nation's fluctuating political fortunes, with all three services fighting for survival in the midst of the worst economic crisis in Britain's history and the politicians' fool's paradise of disarmament, nothing at all had been done to authorize even the modest expansion of the Fleet Air Arm that the Admiralty wanted. The upshot was that of the six aircraft carriers in service at the beginning of 1939, only one, the *Ark Royal* – laid down in 1935 and in the process of completing her trials – was a modern, purpose-built ship. Four of the others were conversions from battleship or battlecruiser hulls and the fifth, HMS *Furious*, was too small to be of much use. Five new 23,370-tonne (23,000-ton) fleet carriers were either under construction or planned; again, it would be 18 months before the first of these was ready for commissioning. As for the first-line aircraft at the Fleet Air Arm's disposal at the beginning of 1939 – the Fairey Swordfish torpedo-bomber, the Blackburn Skua fighter/dive-bomber and the Gloster Sea Gladiator fighter – all were obsolescent.

One predictable result of the Washington Treaty was that all five major maritime powers built cruisers right up to the agreed limit of 10,160 tonnes (10,000 tons), and with the heaviest armament allowed. Britain, for example, laid down seven 'Kent' class ships of 10,038 tonnes (9,880 tons), mounting eight 20cm (8in) guns, followed by six similar 'London' class. A destroyer replacement programme of nine vessels a year, each displacing 1372 tonnes (1350 tons) and mounting four 12cm (4.7in) guns and eight torpedo tubes, was also started in 1929. In addition to this move, the decision was taken to give Britain's ageing submarine force a shot in the arm by building nine 'O' class vessels and six 'P' Class.

By 1930, the strength of the Royal Navy stood at 16 battleships, four battlecruisers, six aircraft carriers, 20 cruisers with 19 or 20cm (7.5 or 8in) armament (with three more building), 40 other cruisers, 146 destroyers (10 more building) and 50 submarines (10 more building). Meanwhile, all the construction programmes of the maritime powers had been severely affected by economic constraints, the world being in the grip of a savage depression. With the exception of Japan, all the maritime nations were eager to escape the cost of building replacement capital ships, as permitted by the Washington Treaty, and on 22 April a new treaty, signed in London by the five principal powers, made fresh provisions. Britain, Japan and the USA agreed that they would lay down no new capital ships before 1936, while France and Italy decided to lay down only the two they were already allowed. Furthermore, the first three countries agreed to make reductions in existing assets; Britain would reduce her force of capital ships to 15 by scrapping HMS *Tiger* and three 'Iron Duke' class vessels, and relegating the old *Iron Duke* herself to the role of training and depot ship. The USA and Japan also agreed to reduce their capital ship assets to 15 and nine respectively.

POTENTIAL THREAT

Within three years, the Treaties of Washington and London had been torn to shreds by the march of international events. First of all, in 1933, Japan invaded Manchuria, giving notice to the world that she intended to establish domination of the Far East, and then withdrew from the League of Nations. She quickly followed this step with a notice to end her adherence to the Washington and London Treaties, her intention being

to establish naval parity with Britain and the USA. France, increasingly alarmed by the growing hostility of fascist Italy, followed suit early in 1935. Also in 1935, and in defiance of the League of Nations, Italy embarked on a campaign of aggression in Abyssinia; and in 1936 Nazi Germany, having repudiated the Treaty of Versailles, seized the Rhineland.

Faced not only with a potential threat to her possessions in the Far East, but also with one much closer to home from a revitalized and increasingly aggressive Germany and an ambitious Italy, Britain began to rearm. Five 'King George V' class fast battleships of 35,562 tonnes (35,000 tons) were laid down, each armed with 10 35.5cm (14in) guns and 16 13cm (5.25in) dual-purpose guns. These were followed, after Japan had abandoned the treaty limits, by four Lion-class ships of 40,642 tonnes (40,000 tons) mounting nine 40.5cm (16in) guns, although the Lions were later cancelled. At the same time, existing British capital ships were modernized with the provision of extra armour and improved armament.

The cruiser force also underwent substantial upgrading. Eight 'Leander' class vessels of 7112 tonnes (7000 tons), armed with eight 15cm (6in) guns were built, followed by four 5304-tonne (5220-ton) Arethusas with six guns. This kept the cruiser tonnage within the limits imposed by the London Treaty, but the subsequent crash rearmament programme produced eight Southamptons of 9246 tonnes (9100 tons) mounting 12 15cm (6in) guns, followed by two slightly larger Edinburghs and 11 'Fiji' class of 8128 tonnes (8000 tons), with the same armament. Eleven 'Dido' class vessels were also laid down; these were 5863-tonne (5770-ton) ships

BELOW: Units of the Home Fleet at anchor on the Thames between Southend and London Bridge for King George V's Silver Jubilee. The aircraft carriers Argus and Courageous are on the left.

with an armament of 10 13cm (5.25in) DP guns, their primary role being to counter air attack. As well as these new warships, the older eight-inch cruisers of post-war vintage were retained in service, as were 23 'C', 'D' and 'E' class vessels. Six of these were rearmed with eight 10cm (4in) AA guns as anti-aircraft cruisers. There were also three surviving 'Hawkins' class cruisers, one of which, HMS *Effingham*, was rearmed with nine 15cm (6in) guns.

Destroyers, too, were key participants in the maritime arms race. In order to keep pace with destroyer developments in other countries, Britain laid down 16 big 'Tribal' class vessels of 1900 tonnes (1870 tons), armed with eight 12cm (4.7in) guns and four torpedo tubes, followed by the 1717-tonne (1690-ton) 'J' and 'K' classes with six 12cm (4.7in) guns and eight torpedo tubes. An entirely new design of small, fast destroyer of 915 tonnes (900 tons) and 58km/h (32kt) was also introduced; this was the 'Hunt' class, 20 of which were on the stocks at the outbreak of war. Although of limited endurance, they were to give excellent service in home waters.

CORVETTE

To bolster trade protection, the Admiralty ordered more vessels of the type known as sloops, which displaced between 1106 and 1270 tonnes (1088 and 1250 tons) and which, although slow, had good endurance. By 1939, 53 of these sloops were in service with the Royal Navy. Finally, a completely new type of small long-endurance vessel, designed on the lines of the whale-catcher and called a corvette, began to be introduced from 1939.

As to planning and strategy, the Royal Navy, because of Great Britain's global responsibilities, faced far more

BELOW: The cruiser HMS Bermuda, *seen here at Simonstown, South Africa, was one of the 'Fiji' class, several of which were launched just before the outbreak of World War II.*

problems than any other major maritime power. It was the Royal Navy which, when war came, would bear the main responsibility for maritime operations in the North Sea and Atlantic, although it was envisaged that the French Navy would have an important part to play in convoy protection on the more southerly Atlantic routes and in hunting down enemy commerce raiders. As to the Mediterranean, this area of operations would be divided between Britain and France,

ABOVE: **The battleship HMS Warspite, pictured after her reconstruction at Portsmouth in 1924–26, when she had her bridge and funnels remodelled and anti-torpedo bulges fitted.**

the French being responsible for the western part and the British the eastern, although there were plans for some French warships to operate under the command of the British Mediterranean Fleet.

The Italian Navy, the Regia Marina, was seen as a formidable threat. It possessed modern battleships and cruisers, a force of over 100 submarines, and was backed up by large numbers of bombers belonging to the Regia Aeronautica, the Italian Air Force. In the face of this threat, the British and French Admiralties took the joint decision that in the event of war, the Mediterranean would be closed to all mercantile traffic bound for the Middle East; this would be diverted round the Cape of Good Hope, an 20,383km (11,005nm) haul necessitating the rapid establishment of shore bases on the east and west coasts of Africa.

The British and French naval planners had little doubt that their combined navies would be more than a match for the Regia Marina, even though its fighting capability was an unknown quantity – for the simple reason that neither the British nor the French had ever fought against it.

What was also unknown was the true state of the Japanese Navy and its maritime air power, on which intelligence was almost completely lacking. In 1939, Japan was adopting an increasingly belligerent stance towards Britain and the United States, but ships could not be spared to bolster the existing force of cruisers and escort vessels – elderly ships,

the most part – responsible for the defence of British interests in the Far East. Japan had not yet allied herself with Germany and Italy, which had concluded a joint offensive-defensive pact known as the Berlin-Rome Axis on 22 May 1939, but there were indications that she might be persuaded to do so; in that event, a plan existed to reinforce the Eastern Fleet by dispatching the bulk of the Mediterranean Fleet to Singapore, leaving operations in the Mediterranean entirely to the French.

Such, in broad outline, was the state of the Royal Navy in August 1939. And then there was the Navy's greatest asset: its manpower. On 1 January 1939, there were 10,000 regular officers and 109,000 men, together with 12,400 officers and men of the Royal Marines. In addition to these were 73,000 officers and men of the Royal Naval Reserve and 6000 Royal Naval Volunteer Reservists. Together, they formed the best-trained and most dedicated cadre of naval personnel in the world. The tragedy was that, at the outbreak of World War II, their training and dedication were not matched by the standard of the ships available to them; and in the first grim years of battle, many lives would be wasted as a consequence of this inadequacy.

CHAPTER 6

WORLD WAR II

On the outbreak of World War II, the Royal Navy was composed of a mixture of old and new ships. Almost half the ships had seen service, or been built, during World War I, and most of the others had been built in accordance with various pre-war restrictive treaties.

At the outbreak of World War II, the principal concern of the British Admiralty was to safeguard the vital merchant convoys upon which Britain relied for her survival. At this early stage of the war, with only a small number of German U-boats at sea, the main threat to these convoys came from commerce raiders – either warships or armed merchant cruisers. One of the most formidable of the enemy warships

ABOVE: The battlecruiser HMS Hood, pictured in 1938. The Hood, once the world's largest warship, was originally constructed as a response to the German 'Mackensen' class of World War I.

LEFT: The 406mm (16in) main armament and the 2-pdr Pompom anti-aircraft batteries of a 'Nelson' class battleship. Anti-aircraft armament was increased as the war progressed.

was the so-called 'pocket battleship' *Admiral Graf Spee*, which was operating against merchant ships in the South Atlantic. A massive search for her was initiated, and among the British warships allocated to it were three cruisers whose names were to become famous: the *Achilles*, *Ajax* and *Exeter*. Early in December 1939 these ships were on station off the River Plate, where there was a great deal of mercantile traffic. The officer in overall command of the British vessels, Commodore Henry Harwood, reasoned that the concentration of shipping would attract the *Graf Spee*, and he was right.

After sinking two more ships in mid-ocean, the *Graf Spee*'s captain, Hans Langsdorff, elected to steer directly for the Plate estuary, where she was sighted at 0608 on 13 December. The three British cruisers were soon in action against her, opening fire from different directions.

Langsdorff at first divided his armament, but then concentrated his fire on the *Exeter*, his 28cm (11in) shells inflicting heavy damage on the cruiser. Despite this, Captain F.S. Bell continued to engage the enemy throughout the night, at the end of which the *Exeter* had only one turret left in action and she was ablaze. Langsdorff could easily have finished her off; instead, he made smoke and turned west, allowing *Exeter* to pull away to the southeast to make repairs, with 61 of her crew dead and 23 wounded.

The pocket battleship now steered for the coast of Uruguay, under fire all the while from the light cruisers *Ajax* and *Achilles*. At 0725, a 28cm (11in) shell hit *Ajax* and put both her after-turrets out of action, but again Langsdorff failed to take the opportunity to finish off one of his adversaries, whose remaining guns were now barely superior to his own secondary armament. The two cruisers continued to shadow the *Graf Spee*, which fired salvoes at them from time to time, until the battleship entered the estuary. Commodore

Harwood then called off the pursuit and set up a patrol line, aware that he was in a very parlous position if Langsdorff chose to fight his way out to the open sea.

SCUTTLED

Langsdorff, his ship damaged – she had taken some 70 hits and 36 of her crew were dead, with another 60 wounded – had decided to make for a neutral port where he could effect temporary repairs before attempting a breakout into the North Atlantic and a run back to Germany. He was also short of ammunition.

The *Graf Spee* reached Montevideo on the evening of 14 December, and there now began a prolonged diplomatic effort to remain in port beyond the legal limit of 72 hours, since the necessary repairs would take an estimated two weeks to complete. The German gamble failed. The necessary authority to remain in port was not forthcoming, and the *Admiral Graf Spee* was scuttled in the River Plate estuary after her crew had disembarked. Langsdorff committed suicide.

Of the three cruisers that had hounded the German warship to its destruction, the *Exeter* was lost on 1 March 1942, sunk by Japanese warships in the Battle of the South Java Sea. The *Ajax* went on to serve with the Mediterranean Fleet and survived the war, being scrapped in 1949. The *Achilles* – which was then serving with the Royal New Zealand Navy – subsequently served with the British Home Fleet and the Pacific Fleet; she was later transferred to the Royal Indian Navy and renamed *Delhi*.

In May 1941, cruisers also played a key part in the hunting and destruction of the battleship *Bismarck*, heading into the North Atlantic with her consort, the heavy cruiser *Prinz Eugen*. Commanded by Admiral Günther Lütjens, the two ships formed a powerful battle group, presenting the biggest threat so far to the Atlantic convoys. The pursuit of the *Bismarck* involved a gigantic cooperative effort by all types of Royal Navy warship, and is worth examining in detail.

As soon as he learned that the German warships had broken out, Admiral Sir John Tovey, commanding the British Home Fleet, sailed from Scapa Flow to join the heavy cruisers *Norfolk* and *Suffolk*, patrolling the Denmark Strait. Three more cruisers were patrolling Lütjens's alternative break-out route, between Iceland and the Faeroes. First to arrive were the Home Fleet's two fastest ships, the battleship *Prince of Wales* and the battlecruiser *Hood*. Behind them came the *King George V*, four cruisers, nine destroyers, and the new aircraft carrier *Victorious*, which had sailed into Scapa Flow from her exercises a day earlier.

At 1915 on 23 May, a young lookout on HMS *Suffolk*, Able Seaman Newall, sighted the enemy ships off the ice shelf

LEFT: The 'Southampton' class cruiser HMS Sheffield served with the Home Fleet and with Force H at Gibraltar. She played a key part in the hunt for the Bismarck *in May 1941.*

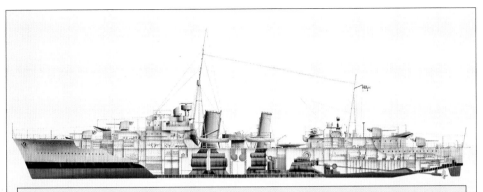

One of the best known of the 'Tribal' class destroyers, HMS Cossack led the destroyer force that rescued British merchant seamen from the Altmark in Narvik Fjord, February 1940. She was lost in October 1941, foundering under tow 100 miles west of Gibraltar after being torpedoed by the U563.

between Iceland and Greenland. *Suffolk's* captain, Robert Ellis, ordered hard-a-port and full speed ahead, making for the safety of a fog bank as the battleship bore down on him less than 13km (7nm) away. He waited for the *Bismarck's* first shattering salvo. It never came.

The *Suffolk* ran through the fog, her radar keeping track of the enemy ships as they passed her. Ellis held his course for 24km (13nm) and then swung out of the fog, taking up station in the wake of the *Prinz Eugen*. By now *Norfolk* was already coming up fast, having picked up her sister ship's signals, and she emerged from the fog to find *Bismarck* only 9.65km (six miles ahead), coming straight at her. The cruiser's captain, Alfred Phillips, at once ordered a turn to starboard, and at that moment the battleship opened fire.

A few moments later, *Norfolk* was surrounded by great geysers of water. Shell splinters whined through the air; some ricocheted off the cruiser's decks, but caused no damage or casualties. The cruiser reached the sanctuary of the fog bank and Phillips took similar action to his counterpart, keeping his ship concealed until she was a safe distance away, before re-emerging to trail *Suffolk*.

It was a long night, and throughout it the pursuit continued through patches of fog and squalls of snow. *Prinz Eugen* was now in the lead, having overtaken *Bismarck* when the latter's electronic steering gear temporarily jammed, causing her to heel over to starboard. The shadowing cruisers were between 18 and 26km (9.7 and 14nm) astern, all four warships racing on at 30 knots, the cruisers juddering and vibrating as they ploughed on through a peppermint-green sea.

Just before midnight, *Bismarck* disappeared into a snowstorm and the cruisers lost contact with her, both visually and by radar. After a couple of anxious hours, *Suffolk* regained radar contact at 0250, and 30 minutes later, in improving

visibility, she sighted the battleship. The cruiser's visual lookouts were having trouble with mirages, which were producing some extraordinary effects. Once, it seemed that the *Bismarck* had turned round and was heading directly towards them.

FATAL RENDEZVOUS

The four ships were now running southwest through the Denmark Strait, having passed the northwest tip of Iceland, and were steaming parallel with the limit of the pack ice. All the while, the *Hood* and *Prince of Wales* were drawing closer to a fatal rendezvous. In the cruisers, excitement mounted. Their crews had been unaware that British heavy warships were racing into action until 0445, when they intercepted a signal from an accompanying destroyer. Thirty minutes later, *Norfolk's* lookouts sighted two smudges of smoke on the port bow, and a few minutes later they made out the shapes of the *Hood* and *Prince of Wales*. The German warships were also in sight, 30km (16nm) off the port bow. The men on the cruisers were about to have a grandstand view of the coming battle. Little did they realise what they were about to witness.

At 0553, the opposing forces opened fire almost simultaneously. Great orange flashes and huge clouds of black smoke belched from the forward turrets of the *Hood* as she fired her first salvo. It fell just astern of the *Bismarck*, sending fountains of water 61m (200ft) into the air. The German battleship's salvo was still coming in.

For the ship that had been the Royal Navy's pride, the end came swiftly. Two shell splashes rose beside her, and almost immediately the horrified spectators on the *Prince of Wales* saw a vast eruption of flame leap upwards from between her masts, accompanied by a great incandescent fireball.

ABOVE: The battleships HMS Malaya and Ramillies, with the cruiser HMS Kent in the background, en route to bombard Bardia and Fort Capuzzo in Cyrenaica on the morning of 17 August 1940.

The volcanic burst of fire lasted only a second or two, and when it disappeared, the space that had been occupied by the *Hood* was obscured by a great column of smoke. Through it, the bows and stern of the ship could just be seen, each rising steeply up as the central part of the ship collapsed. Within a minute or so she was gone, taking with her all but three of her complement of 1416 officers and men, including the force commander, Vice-Admiral Lancelot Holland.

The destruction of the *Hood* had left Admiral Lütjens free to concentrate his warships' fire on the British battleship, and in 10 minutes she was hit by four 38cm (15in) and three 20cm (8in) shells. One 38cm (15in) missile wrecked her bridge, killing or wounding everyone except Captain John Leach and his Chief Yeoman of Signals. Apart from the human carnage they caused, the shells severed communications to the steering wheel and destroyed some of the gunnery control telephone leads.

Another 38cm (15in) shell hit the superstructure supporting the gun directors that controlled the forward secondary armament of 14cm (5.5in) guns and put them out of action. A third hit smashed the wings of the ship's spotter aircraft, which was on the point of being catapulted off; the crew scrambled clear and the dangerous, fuel-laden wreck was tipped over the side. Yet another heavy shell had penetrated the side deep under water, passing through several bulkheads and coming to rest without exploding near the diesel dynamo room. It was only discovered after the battleship returned to harbour. Two of the 20cm (8in) shells had pierced the ship's side aft, on the waterline, allowing 508 tones (500 tons) of water to pour into the ship. The third entered one of the 13.3cm (5.25in) shell handling rooms, bounced around the confined space like a streak of lightning, then fell to the floor, also without exploding. By some miracle, no one was hurt. With five of his 35cm (14in) guns out of action, and the range down to 13,267m (14,500yds), Captain Leach had no choice but to break off the engagement.

OIL LEAKAGE

Lütjens, at that moment, might well have decided to close in and finish off the *Prince of Wales*, but he had no notion of the damage his battleship had inflicted on her. Besides, he had problems of his own. The exchange of gunfire had not been entirely one-sided. The *Prince of Wales* had fired 18 salvoes, and one of them had found its mark. *Bismarck* had been hit by three shells, one of which caused an oil leakage from two fuel tanks, and the contamination of others by sea water. At 0800, the German admiral decided to abandon his sortie into the Atlantic and head for St Nazaire, the only port on the Atlantic coast with a dry dock big enough to take his flagship. He would detach *Prinz Eugen* en route, to make her way to Brest alone. Still shadowed by the cruisers, the *Bismarck* ploughed on, leaving a tell-tale slick of oil behind her.

A Hudson aircraft from Iceland had observed the brief battle. It now circled the spot where the *Hood* had gone down, directing destroyers to the scene. The rescuers found three Carley rafts close together, each with an exhausted, shell-shocked man clinging to it. They were Midshipman Dundas, Able Seaman Tilburn, and Signalman Briggs.

The destroyers searched for a long time, the rescuers wondering what had happened to the rest of *Hood*'s crew. It was only slowly that the realisation dawned on them. There were only three survivors.

A formidable array of warships was now converging on the *Bismarck*. As well as Admiral Somerville's Force H, coming up

SOME OF THE SHIPS THAT HUNTED THE BISMARCK

HMS Suffolk. A 'Kent' class cruiser displacing 9,957 tonnes (9,800 tons), *Suffolk* was launched at Portsmouth in February 1926. She carried a complement of 679 and was armed with eight 20cm (8in) and eight 10cm (4in) guns, a variety of anti-aircraft weapons and eight 53cm (21in) torpedo tubes. Her four-shaft geared turbines gave her a top speed of 31 knots. *Suffolk* served with the Home Fleet until 1943, when she was transferred to the Eastern Fleet. She was scrapped at Newport in June 1948.

HMS Norfolk and HMS Dorsetshire. Cruisers of the same class, these ships were of the same displacement and carried the same armament as *Suffolk*. *Norfolk* was launched at Fairfield in December 1928 and *Dorsetshire* at Portsmouth in January 1929. Both ships had a complement of 650 and a top speed of 32 knots. *Norfolk* served with the Home Fleet throughout the war and was scrapped at Newport in February 1950; *Dorsetshire* was transferred to the Eastern Fleet and was sunk by Japanese air attack off Ceylon on 5 April 1942.

HMS Sheffield. A cruiser of the 'Southampton' class displacing 9,246 tonnes (9,100 tons), *Sheffield* was launched on the Tyne in July 1946. She had a complement of 700 and her main armament comprised twelve 15cm (6in) guns. She also carried an anti-aircraft armament of eight 10cm (4in) and eight pom-pom guns, the same as the cruisers described above. Maximum speed was 32 knots. Apart from a brief spell with Force H at Gibraltar in 1940–41, *Sheffield* served with the Home Fleet throughout the war. She was scrapped at Inverkeithing in September 1967.

HMS Prince of Wales. A battleship of the 'King George V' class, the *Prince of Wales* was launched in March 1939. Displacing 35,560 tonnes (35,000 tons), she had a complement of 1,550. Main armament was ten 35cm (14in) guns, backed up by 16 13cm (5.25in) dual purpose guns and 48 pom-poms (six batteries of eight). Maximum speed was 27 knots. The *Prince of Wales* was transferred to the Eastern Fleet to reinforce Singapore and was sunk on 10 December 1941 by a Japanese air attack off the coast of Malaya, together with the battlecruiser *Repulse*.

HMS King George V. Launched on the Tyne in February 1939, the 'KG V' served mostly with the Home Fleet, but operated in support of the Allied landings in Sicily in 1943,

together with her sister ship HMS *Howe*. She served with the Pacific Fleet in 1945 and was scrapped in 1958–59. Details as for *Prince of Wales*.

HMS Rodney. One of two battleships in the 'Nelson' class, *Rodney* displaced 34,495 tonnes (33,950 tons) and had a complement of 1,314. Her two-shaft geared turbines gave her a top speed of 23 knots. Main armament was nine 40cm (16in) guns, supported by 12 15cm (6in) guns. Anti-aircraft armament comprised six 12cm (4.7in) and 24 Bofors guns. *Rodney* served throughout the war with the Home Fleet, except for a period supporting Allied operations in the Mediterranean in 1943. She was scrapped at Inverkeithing in March 1948.

HMS Ark Royal. Launched in April 1937, the aircraft carrier *Ark Royal* displaced 28,165 tonnes (27,720 tons) fully laden and had a complement of 1575. She could carry a maximum of 60 aircraft and was capable of over 30 knots. Armament comprised 16 11.4cm (4.5in) dual-purpose guns, and 48 pom-poms (six batteries of eight). She operated with the Home Fleet during the Norwegian Campaign before being transferred to Force H at Gibraltar in support of operations in the Mediterranean, notably the Malta convoys. She was torpedoed by the *U81* on 13 November 1941 and sank under tow the next day.

HMS Victorious. One of the 'Illustrious' class, the aircraft carrier *Victorious* was launched on the Tyne in September 1939. Displacing 29,078 tonnes (28,619 tons) fully laden, she had a complement of 2,200 and an armoured hangar, reducing the size of her air group to 36 aircraft. After modification, this was later increased to 72. Armament as for *Ark Royal*, modified later to 12 7.62cm (3in) and six 40mm AA guns. *Victorious* served in all theatres of the war and took part in raids on the Japanese Home Islands in 1945. She was rebuilt in 1950–57 and was broken up at Faslane in 1969, having been damaged by fire two years earlier.

HMS Cossack. A 'Tribal' class destroyer, *Cossack* was launched on the Tyne in June 1937. Displacing 1,900 tonnes (1,870 tons), she had a complement of 219. Main armament was eight 12cm (4.7in) guns and four AA pom-pom guns. She had four 53cm (21in) torpedo tubes. Maximum speed was 36 knots. *Cossack* was torpedoed by the *U563* in the North Atlantic on 23 October 1941 and foundered west of Gibraltar four days later.

*ABOVE: **The battleship** Bismarck **firing a salvo at HMS** Hood. **The flash of the guns makes this look like a nighttime shot, but it is daylight. The photo was taken from the cruiser** Prinz Eugen.*

from Gibraltar to cut off the German commander's escape route to the south, and Admiral Tovey's force, the battleships *Rodney* and *Ramillies* were also released from escort duties to take part in the chase, while the cruisers *Edinburgh* and *Dorsetshire* were detached from escort work to join the other cruisers shadowing the enemy. The main concern now was to reduce the *Bismarck*'s speed, giving the hunters a chance to close in for the kill – and that was where the *Victorious* and her aircraft came in. At 1440 hours on 24 May, Admiral Tovey had sent the aircraft carrier racing ahead of the main force to try and reach a position from which she could fly off her Swordfish aircraft against the *Bismarck*. If they could reach her, they might slow her down.

*LEFT: **Painting showing the destruction of the** Hood **in the** Denmark Strait, **with the** Prince of Wales **bypassing the wreckage. Only three men survived out of a total of 1341.***

FALSE TRAIL

At 2210 the carrier flew off nine Swordfish of No 825 Squadron, led by Lieutenant Commander Eugene Esmonde. Flying through rain and sleet, they obtained radar contact with the enemy at 2337 and briefly sighted the *Bismarck*, only to lose her again. Twenty minutes later, the shadowing British cruisers redirected the Swordfish on to their target and they made their attack through heavy defensive fire. One torpedo hit the *Bismarck* amidships without causing significant damage; the other eight missed. All the attacking Swordfish recovered safely to the carrier, although two reconnaissance Fulmars out of six dispatched failed to return. The returning crews reported no sign of the *Prinz Eugen*, which had in fact been detached by Admiral Lütjens to continue on her way alone.

At 0300 on 25 May, Lütjens altered course to the southeast, and at this critical juncture the shadowing cruisers, which had been following at extreme radar range, lost contact. The problems facing *Bismarck*'s pursuers were compounded by the receipt of some bearings transmitted by the Admiralty which, through a combination of errors, led Admiral Tovey to believe that the battleship was heading northeast, into the Atlantic. As a result, Tovey's flagship and many other pursuing vessels followed this false trail throughout most of 25 May, until, at about 1800, it was decided that the *Bismarck* was probably heading for Brest, and the ships changed course accordingly. A signal received at 1924 indicated that the Admiralty also thought that this was the case; in fact, the Admiralty, much earlier in the day, had already instructed Admiral Somerville's Force H to position itself on a line from which its ships and aircraft could intercept the *Bismarck* should she head for the Bay of Biscay. It turned out to be a fortuitous move and one which would prove decisive in the action.

Although Tovey's warships had lost valuable ground during their false quest to the northeast, the net around *Bismarck* was gradually closing. At 1030 on 26 May, *Bismarck* was sighted nearly 1297km (700nm) west of Brest by a Catalina of No 209 Squadron from Castle Archdale (Lough Erne) in Northern Ireland. Soon after the Catalina crew sighted the *Bismarck*, contact was also made by two Swordfish reconnaissance aircraft from the *Ark Royal*, Force H's aircraft carrier. Admiral Somerville sent the cruiser *Sheffield* to shadow the battleship with her Type 79Y radar and, when the opportunity arose, to direct a strike by the carrier's Swordfish torpedo-bombers. Fourteen of the latter were flown off at 1450 in conditions of high winds, driving rain and rough seas, and some time later their radar revealed a target which their crews assumed was the *Bismarck*. In fact it was the *Sheffield*, whose presence in the area had not been signalled to *Ark Royal*. The Swordfish came down through low cloud and attacked from different directions; several of them released their torpedoes before the mistake was recognised, but fortunately – thanks to a combination of effective evasive manoeuvring by the cruiser and faulty magnetic pistols fitted to the torpedoes – no damage was caused.

At 1910 the carrier launched a second wave of 15 Swordfish. The aircraft, led by Lieutenant Commander T.P. Coode, were directed to the target by the *Sheffield*, but in the prevailing weather conditions, coupled with fading light and heavy defensive fire, they had little chance of making a coordinated attack. Nevertheless, two torpedoes found their mark; one struck the *Bismarck*'s armoured belt and did little damage, but the other struck her extreme stern, damaging her propellers and jamming her rudders 15 degrees to port. At 2140, Admiral Lütjens signalled Berlin; 'Ship no longer manoeuvrable. We fight to the last shell. Long live the Führer.'

STRIKING DISTANCE

Shortly afterwards, five destroyers, led by Captain Philip Vian in the *Cossack*, arrived on the scene, having been detached from convoy duty. They made contact with the *Bismarck* and shadowed her throughout the night, transmitting regular position reports and closing in to make a series of determined torpedo attacks. These were disrupted, however, by heavy and accurate radar-controlled gunfire. Whether any torpedoes hit their target or not is still a mystery; the destroyer crews maintained that they saw two explosions on the *Bismarck*, but the survivors of the battleship later stated that no hits were made. Whatever the truth, the *Bismarck* was seen to reduce speed, so driving a further nail into her own coffin.

During the night, the battleships *King George V* and *Rodney* came within striking distance of their crippled enemy, but Admiral Tovey, aware of the accuracy of her radar-directed gunnery, decided to wait until daylight before engaging her; she had no means of escaping him now.

Soon after dawn on 27 May, he closed in from the northwest, his two battleships opening fire at about 0845 from a range of 14,670m (16,043yds). By 1020 the *Bismarck* had been reduced to a blazing wreck, with all her armament out

A member of a naval gun crew holding a cordite charge. He is wearing a steel helmet and anti-flash protection gear, with asbestos gloves protecting his hands and forearms. Tending a ship's gun battery was hot, sweaty and dangerous, demanding excellent teamwork from those involved.

of action, but she was still afloat despite the fact that the two British battleships had fired over 700 shells at her. Only a small proportion had found their target, prompting Admiral Tovey to tell his fleet gunnery officer that he would stand a better chance of hitting her if he threw his binoculars at her. In the end, the battleships, undamaged but seriously short of fuel, were compelled to break off the action, and it was left to the cruisers *Norfolk* and *Dorsetshire* to close in and finish the *Bismarck* off with torpedoes. She sank at 1036, her colours still flying, in position 48°10'N, 16°12'W, taking all but 119 of her crew of over 2000 officers and men with her.

The Royal Navy, greatly assisted by the Royal Canadian Navy and, from late 1941, by the United States Navy, still had a long and hard road to travel before the Battle of the Atlantic was won. One principal weapon in the British armoury was a knowledge of German naval movements, thanks to the breaking of the Enigma code; the resulting intelligence information, known under the codename Ultra, often enabled convoys to be routed around the German U-boat packs. But there were other, less subtle weapons.

One measure that did give the Allies a considerable advantage in the Atlantic battles of 1942 was the large-scale introduction of shipborne HF/DF (High Frequency Direction Finding) equipment, known as 'Huff-Duff' to those who used it. The wolfpack tactics employed by the U-boats required them to make radio reports to their shore stations when they made or lost contact with a convoy, and a single HF/DF ship could provide reliable detection of a U-boat making a transmission on the frequency the ship was guarding when the latter was within 'ground wave' range 42–48km (15–30 miles). Each HF/DF report enabled the escort commander to send anti-submarine ships, and an escorting aircraft if he had to one, to search for and attack the U-boat. The submarines needed their surface speed to keep up with or overtake a convoy, and even if the searching escorts failed to find and attack the U-boat, they could probably force it to submerge until the convoy was out of sight. By the end of January 1942, 25 escorts had been fitted with HF/DF, and the number increased steadily throughout the year. Next to centimetric radar, HF/DF was probably the most important element in winning the Battle of the Atlantic. In combination with radar, it eventually made submarine attacks on convoys too hazardous to be attempted.

IMMENSE STRAIN

In 1942, though, despite the growing number of Allied surface and air escorts, and despite the introduction of new equipment, merchant shipping losses mounted to unprecedented levels. In November they reached an all-time record of 711,235 tonnes (700,000 tons). The Germans were now suffering severe reverses in the Soviet Union and North Africa, and the Atlantic seemed the one area in which they could inflict terrible damage on the Allies. With Allied shipping under immense strain the outlook was bleak, and when the figures for 1942 were added up, they reached the appalling total of 1664 merchantmen – nearly 8,128,400

BELOW: The 38cm (15in) guns of HMS Valiant *firing a broadside. The battleships HMS* Barham *and HMS* Warspite *are in the background.* Barham *was sunk by the* U331 *in November 1941.*

tonnes (8,000,000 tons) – lost on the high seas. Unless this rate of loss could be reduced, there seemed no prospect that the construction of new merchant tonnage could outstrip sinkings, and the gloomy economic news was that Britain's imports had fallen to two-thirds of the 1939 total.

But the tide was about to turn. In March 1943, as the Atlantic battles raged, representatives of the British, American and Canadian navies met in an 'Atlantic Convoy Conference' in Washington. It was agreed that the US Navy should assume responsibility for the tanker convoys running between Britain and the West Indies, leaving the North Atlantic entirely to the British and Canadians. The Royal Canadian Navy, directed by a new Northwest Atlantic Command HQ at Halifax, would be entirely responsible for the North Atlantic convoys as far as 47°W, where the Royal Navy would take over. March also saw the formation of the first Support Groups, which would provide rapid reinforcement for convoys under threat. Two of the first five were composed of destroyers drawn from the Home Fleet, two of escort vessels from the Western Approaches Command, all with highly experienced crews, and the fifth was formed around the escort carrier HMS *Biter*.

From early 1942, much of the Royal Navy's effort was devoted to protecting the convoys to the Soviet Union from attacks not only by U-boats and aircraft, but from the threat of attack by heavy naval units such as the new battleship *Tirpitz* and the heavy cruisers *Lützow*, *Admiral Scheer*, *Admiral Hipper* and the battlecruiser *Scharnhorst*, which had been deployed to Norwegian bases. By December 1943, when the *Scharnhorst* was sunk by units of the Home Fleet off Norway's North Cape, this threat was greatly reduced; other heavy units had been redeployed to the Baltic and the *Tirpitz*, damaged by air and midget submarine attack, remained penned up in her Norwegian lair until she was sunk by the RAF in November 1944.

In the Mediterranean theatre, the British Fleet was built around the older 'Queen Elizabeth' class battleships: the *Barham*, *Malaya*, *Queen Elizabeth*, *Valiant* and *Warspite*. The *Barham* was an early casualty. On 25 November 1941, she was hit by three torpedoes from the U331 and exploded with the loss of 862 lives. In the following month, the *Queen Elizabeth* and *Valiant* were both badly damaged in a daring attack by Italian frogmen as they lay in Alexandria harbour; neither would play an active part in the war thereafter.

It was the aircraft carrier that was to play a key part in the struggle for naval supremacy in the Mediterranean, beginning with the devastating attack on the Italian fleet at Taranto by Swordfish aircraft from HMS *Illustrious* in

ABOVE: **HMS King George V** *pictured in 1941. The 'KG V' served with the Home Fleet and in the Pacific, where her heavy armament proved invaluable for shore bombardment.*

November 1940. Without aircraft carriers, flying off vital reinforcement aircraft and protecting supply convoys, the strategic island of Malta could not have survived. At no time did the prospects of its survival look grimmer than in August 1942, when the Admiralty mounted Operation Pedestal, a desperate, do-or-die attempt to relieve the island. On 10 August, 13 freighters and the tanker *Ohio* passed into the Mediterranean en route for Malta. To support the convoy, every available warship had been assembled. The escort and covering force included the carriers *Victorious*, *Indomitable*, and *Eagle*, the battleships *Nelson* and *Rodney*, seven cruisers (three anti-aircraft) and 25 destroyers. The convoy also included the old carrier *Furious*, which was to accompany the main body to a point 150 miles west of Malta and fly off 38 badly needed Spitfires.

FORMIDABLE ODDS

The convoy was sailing into the teeth of formidable odds. On airfields in Sardinia and Italy, the Germans and Italians had massed nearly 800 aircraft. Across the convoy's route, between Gibraltar and the Narrows, 19 enemy submarines were lying in wait. In the Sicilian Channel, a force of cruisers, destroyers and MTBs was lurking, ready to attack under cover of darkness after the main escort had turned away.

The first day passed fairly quietly. On the carriers, the fighter pilots remained at readiness and the crews of the torpedo aircraft helped to man the ships' guns. Early on 11 August, however, the first Junkers 88 reconnaissance aircraft appeared and circled the convoy at a respectful distance. The *Indomitable* sent up two flights of Sea Hurricanes of Nos 800 and 880 Squadrons to try to intercept the shadowers, but the Ju 88s easily outpaced their pursuers. Then, at 1316, a series

ABOVE: *The 'S', 'T' and 'U' classes of British submarine accounted for most of the Royal navy's submersible craft during World War II. Seen here is HMS Seraph, launched in October 1941.*

of explosions reverberated through the convoy. For a few moments nobody knew quite what had happened; then the *Eagle* was seen to be listing and shrouded in smoke. She had been hit by four torpedoes from the submarine *U73*. The other ships of the escort immediately increased speed and began to take evasive action, depth-charging at random. Just eight minutes later, the *Eagle* had gone, taking 160 of her crew to the bottom with her; 759 were rescued, and four Sea Hurricanes of No 801 Squadron which had been on combat air patrol landed on the fleet carriers.

The loss of the old carrier was a bitter blow; during her time in the Mediterranean, she had dispatched 185 fighters to Malta, quietly and without the publicity that had attended some of the other carrier reinforcement operations. She had become synonymous with the island's survival.

Minutes after the *Eagle* had sunk, the white track of a torpedo crossed the bow of the *Victorious*. As the convoy continued to take evasive action, a submarine was sighted and the escorts raced off to unload their depth charges on it, but without any visible result. In all, six submarine sightings were reported in the hours that followed.

Shortly before sunset the *Furious* flew off her Spitfires and turned back towards Gibraltar, her mission completed, escorted by five reserve destroyers. Soon afterwards, as dusk was falling, the convoy was subjected to its first air attack by 36 Ju 88s and He 111s which dropped their bombs and escaped before the defending fighters could engage them, except for three which were shot down by AA fire. None of the ships was hit.

First light on 12 August revealed a pair of SM 79s shadowing the convoy. Both were shot down by 809 Squadron's Fulmars. It was a good start to the day, but everyone knew that the real test was still to come. The convoy was now coming well within range of enemy airfields, and the bombers that came that day would undoubtedly have fighter escorts. The first raid materialised at 0900, when a formation of 20 Ju 88s appeared at 2440m (8000ft). They were intercepted by the *Indomitable*'s Hurricanes, which shot down two on their

first pass and forced several others to jettison their bombs. More Hurricanes and Fulmars from the *Victorious* arrived a couple of minutes later and joined the fray, destroying four more bombers and driving the others away.

After two more small and unsuccessful attacks that morning, a really big raid appeared at noon. Nearly 100 bombers, with a strong fighter escort, were hotly engaged by every available Fleet Air Arm fighter as they approached the convoy. Harried by the fighters, the enemy formations became dislocated while still some distance from the target. The only real damage was caused by a formation of Ju 88s that broke through the fighter screen and dive-bombed the freighter *Deucalion*; badly damaged, the vessel began to lag behind the rest of the convoy and had to be left, escorted by the destroyer *Bramham*. She was attacked and sunk before dusk by two torpedo-bombers.

That afternoon, the convoy ran into a submarine ambush laid by the Italian Navy. One submarine, the *Cobalto*, was brought to the surface by depth charges and rammed by the destroyer *Ithuriel*, which was herself badly damaged. None of the torpedoes launched by the submarines scored hits. The convoy was under continual air attack throughout the afternoon, but emerged relatively unharmed. By 1700, however, the ships were within range of Fliegerkorps II's dive-bombers in Sicily, and from now on the attacks were pressed home with great determination. For two hours the bombers came over without pause, allowing the exhausted Navy pilots no respite. Part of a formation of 29 Ju 87s of StG3, harried by Fulmars and Martlets (nine of which were operated by *Indomitable*'s No 806 Squadron) broke through and dropped three bombs on the carrier. They failed to penetrate her flight deck, but for the time being she could not operate her aircraft, and those of her fighters still airborne had to land on the *Victorious*. An attack was also made by 14 SM 79s, which torpedoed the destroyer *Foresight*; she had to be abandoned and sunk later.

NAVY PILOTS

By 1930 the last of the raiders had disappeared; the convoy was still more or less intact and was now only 240km (130nm) from Malta, within range of the island's Beaufighters. The first of these arrived overhead as dusk was falling, and the two fleet carriers, their job done, now turned away towards the sunset.

They had lost 13 of their aircraft, but their pilots had claimed 39 enemy aircraft definitely destroyed during the three days of air fighting, plus a further nine probables. It had been a classic demonstration of the value of carrier-borne fighters. The Navy pilots had ably proved their ability to break up even the most determined enemy attacks, and the fact that the convoy had come this far without suffering serious harm was due in large measure to them. Now, however, the carriers had turned for home, leaving the convoy to steam on through the night with only the scant air cover that could be provided by the RAF on Malta. And the story of 13 August was to be tragically different from that of the three preceding days.

During the night, the convoy was repeatedly attacked by enemy MTBs and submarines, followed up by a savage air onslaught that lasted until the surviving ships reached Malta. Only four of the merchantmen – including the vital tanker *Ohio* – got through, and the escort suffered the loss of the cruisers *Cairo* and *Manchester*. Nevertheless, the supplies that did get through enabled the island to keep going until November, when relief reached the defenders following the Allied landings in North Africa and the Eighth Army's decisive victory over Rommel at El Alamein. And in the summer of 1943, it was Malta that provided a principal base when the Allies stormed ashore on Sicily.

The first year of the Royal Navy's war in the Far East, following the Japanese attack on Pearl Harbor and the invasion of Malaya, was a lengthy catalogue of disaster. First, on 10 December 1941, came the sinking of the battleship *Prince of Wales* and the battlecruiser *Repulse* off the coast of Malaya. Then, in February 1942, came the Battle of the Java Sea, which saw the loss of several British warships including the cruiser *Exeter*, veteran of the Battle of the River Plate.

In the spring of 1942, while the victorious Japanese consolidated their lightning conquests in Southeast Asia and the Pacific, the British Admiralty focused its attention on

*BELOW: **The aircraft carrier HMS** Victorious **saw action in every theatre of the war, from the Arctic to the Pacific, where her aircraft took part in raids on Japan.***

constructing a new Eastern Fleet to operate from Ceylon, the base the Admiralty had recommended in the first place. By the end of March, the new Eastern Fleet comprised two large aircraft carriers, the *Indomitable* and *Formidable*, (the latter operational once more after a 10-month break following the damage she had sustained off Crete in May 1941) and a small one, the *Hermes*; five battleships, the *Ramillies, Resolution, Revenge, Royal Sovereign* and *Warspite*, all of World War I vintage; seven cruisers, 16 destroyers and seven submarines. The Fleet was commanded, from 27 March, by Admiral Sir James Somerville, the able and experienced former commander of Gibraltar's Force H.

DANGEROUS MOMENT

Somerville faced an immediate crisis. On 4 April, a Catalina flying boat sighted a Japanese task force approaching Ceylon from the south and radioed its position minutes before it was shot down. The enemy force was Admiral Nagumo's 1st Carrier Striking Force, comprising the aircraft carriers *Akagi, Hiryu, Shokaku, Soryu* and *Zuikaku* – the ships whose aircraft had wrought such havoc on Pearl Harbor and Port Darwin – accompanied by four battleships, three cruisers and nine destroyers. Between them, the five carriers mustered some 300 strike aircraft and fighters; Admiral Somerville's air assets consisted of 57 strike aircraft and 40 fighters on his carriers, with the Fulmars Nos 803 and 806 Squadrons based ashore at Ratmalana. There were also 50-odd RAF Hurricanes delivered by *Indomitable* on a second ferry run to the Indian Ocean.

The Japanese intention was clearly to destroy the Eastern Fleet. For the British this was a most dangerous move; for all they knew the Japanese might then try to seize the island, from where not only India but also the ocean supply routes to the Middle East could be threatened. This was at a time when all supplies had to be routed around the Cape; Rommel was

ABOVE: *The escort carrier HMS* Biter *and an Atlantic convoy, seen from a Grumman Avenger of No 846 Squadron. Escort carriers were crucial to the survival of Allied convoys.*

driving the Eighth Army back towards Egypt, and a new German offensive was building in the Soviet Union. The possibility of a German-Japanese link-up in the Middle East seems far-fetched with hindsight, but it was of very real concern to Churchill and his colleagues. Later, he was to call it the most dangerous moment of the war.

As soon as the news of the approaching Japanese task force was received, Admiral Layton, the naval commander at Ceylon, ordered every ship that could do so to sail from Colombo harbour. The cruisers *Cornwall* and *Dorsetshire*, which had been detached earlier on Somerville's instructions, were also ordered to rejoin Force A, the fast group of the Eastern Fleet which included the aircraft carriers and the *Warspite*.

FIERCE AIR BATTLES

Early on 5 April – Easter Sunday – the Japanese fleet was sighted by a second Catalina, and soon afterwards it launched a strike of 53 Nakajima B5N Kate high-level bombers and 38 Aichi D3A Val dive-bombers, escorted by 36 Zero fighters, to attack Colombo. Fierce air battles developed over the city and harbour as the raiding force was intercepted by 42 Hurricanes and Fulmars; seven Japanese aircraft were destroyed, but 19 British fighters were shot down. The Zeros also pounced on a luckless formation of six 814 Squadron Swordfish, on their way from Trincomalee to Minneriya, and shot them all out of the sky. The attack caused heavy damage to built-up areas; the damage to shipping and the port installations was relatively light, although the auxiliary cruiser *Hector* and the destroyer *Tenedos* were sunk.

At about noon, the cruisers *Cornwall* and *Dorsetshire* were sighted by a reconnaissance aircraft from the heavy cruiser

Tone and 53 Val dive-bombers were immediately sent out to attack them. The bombing was devastatingly accurate and both ships were sunk, 1112 men (of a total of 1546) being rescued later by the cruiser HMS *Enterprise* and two destroyers. Albacores from the *Indomitable* later made a night radar search for the enemy force, but it had withdrawn to the southeast to refuel before heading back north to strike at Trincomalee naval base. At this time Admiral Somerville's Force A was steaming towards Ceylon from Addu Atoll, with his slow division (Force B) a long way behind; his ships were at times only 370km (200nm) from Nagumo's task force, but neither side made contact with the other. Addu Atoll had been set up as the Eastern Fleet's secret base, and Somerville, unable to locate the enemy, turned back towards it to safeguard it against a possible surprise attack.

On 8 April, a Catalina once again established contact with the Japanese carrier force 740km (400nm) to the east of Ceylon and the ships at Trincomalee were ordered to put to sea. All units – including the light carrier *Hermes* – were able to get clear before the expected attack by 91 high-level and dive-bombers, escorted by 38 fighters, developed early on 9 April. Of the 23 Hurricane and Fulmar fighters sent up to defend the harbour, nine were shot down, as were five out of a formation of nine Blenheim bombers sent out to try to locate the enemy force. Only light damage was inflicted on the target, but on the way back to their ships the Japanese aircrews sighted several ships, including the *Hermes*, the Australian destroyer *Vampire*, the corvette *Hollyhock* and two tankers. Three hours later, 80 dive-bombers arrived on the scene and sank all three warships and the tankers about 65 miles from Trincomalee. The *Hermes*, which had no aircraft on board, radioed desperately for help, but the surviving fighters at Trincomalee were in no position to offer it.

Fortunately perhaps for the Eastern Fleet (whose Force A deployed to Bombay immediately after the attacks on Ceylon, and Force B to East Africa to protect the convoy route), a Japanese task force never again made an appearance in the Indian Ocean. Instead, Admiral Nagumo withdrew to the Pacific in readiness for the next big venture: the occupation of Midway Island. In the event, it proved to be a costly exercise, for during the Battle of Midway on 4–5 June 1942, the carriers *Akagi*, *Kaga*, *Hiryu* and *Soryu* were all sunk by US naval aircraft.

The failure of the Japanese Naval Command to exploit its advantage in the Indian Ocean gave the British Eastern Fleet a breathing space in which to reorganize, but it was not until October 1943, after a break of nine months, that a British aircraft carrier was again deployed to the Indian Ocean. She was the escort carrier HMS *Battler*, and she formed the nucleus of an anti-submarine group which, during the early months of 1944, began hunter-killer operations against the German and Japanese submarines which were preying on shipping in the area from their main base at Penang.

PACIFIC FLEET

At the end of 1943, the British Eastern Fleet – apart from the carrier mentioned above – was reduced to the battleship *Ramillies*, eight cruisers, two auxiliary cruisers, 11 destroyers, 13 frigates, sloops and corvettes and six submarines. It therefore came as a welcome event when, on 30 January 1944, the British naval presence in the Indian Ocean was strengthened by the arrival at Colombo of the battleships *Queen Elizabeth* and *Valiant*, the battlecruiser *Renown*, the carriers *Illustrious* and *Unicorn*, two cruisers and seven destroyers, the whole force having made a fast passage through the Mediterranean after leaving Scapa Flow and the Clyde a month earlier. The first operation by the strengthened Eastern Fleet was a sweep against enemy blockade runners and warships of the 7th Japanese Cruiser Squadron, two of which – the *Kuma* and *Kitakami* – were sunk by submarines in February. Not long afterwards, on 12 March 1944, came the first success of *Battler's* hunter-killer group, when the Fairey Swordfish of No 842 Squadron located an enemy submarine supply ship off the Seychelles and steered destroyers to her position. The loss of this ship, together with another which had been destroyed a fortnight earlier, drastically reduced the time that could be spent at sea by enemy submarines, with a consequent reduction in the tonnage of Allied shipping sunk.

The arrival of powerful warships in the Indian Ocean enabled the British to mount the first of a series of large-scale air attacks, supported by surface bombardment, on Japanese targets – mainly airfields and fuel storage facilities – in the Bay of Bengal, Java and Sumatra. At the end of August 1944, the Eastern Fleet comprised the battleships *Howe*, *Richelieu*, *Queen Elizabeth*, the battlecruiser *Renown*, the carriers *Indomitable* and *Victorious*, 11 cruisers and 32 destroyers. The *Howe* had joined the fleet on 8 August; ironically, on the same day, the *Valiant* was badly damaged in the collapse of the floating dock at Trincomalee. For the time being, then, the Eastern Fleet still had three battleships at its disposal instead of the planned four.

In November 1944, the Eastern Fleet was reorganized, part of it becoming the British East Indies Fleet under Vice-Admiral Sir Arthur Power. It comprised the battleship *Queen Elizabeth*, the battlecruiser *Renown*, five escort carriers, eight cruisers and 24 destroyers. The more modern warships were assigned to the British Pacific Fleet under Admiral Sir Bruce Fraser and included the battleships *King George V* and *Howe*,

the carriers *Indefatigable*, *Illustrious*, *Indomitable* and *Victorious*, the cruisers *Swiftsure*, *Argonaut*, *Black Prince*, *Ceylon*, *Newfoundland*, *Gambia* and *Achilles*, and three destroyer flotillas.

On 16 January 1945, the British Pacific Fleet, as Task Force 87, sailed from Trincomalee for Sydney in the first stage of its planned deployment to the Pacific theatre. It comprised the battleship *King George V* and the carriers *Indefatigable*, *Illustrious*, *Indomitable* and *Victorious*, three cruisers and nine destroyers. En route to Australia, the Fleet's carrier aircraft carried out heavy attacks on Japanese oil targets in Sumatra.

From Sydney, the British Pacific Fleet deployed to its operational base at Ulithi Atoll in the Caroline Islands, where – as Task Force 57 – it formed part of the US Fifth Fleet. In March 1945, it formed part of the naval force covering the American landings on Okinawa, where its carriers were subjected to Kamikaze suicide attacks; time and again, they were saved from serious damage by their armoured flight decks. Operations continued until the end of the Pacific war, culminating in attacks on Japanese warships sheltering in anchorages in the Japanese Home Islands.

SUBMARINES IN THE INDIAN OCEAN

Although British submarine operations in the North Sea and the Mediterranean are well documented, those in the Indian Ocean are less so. By mid-1944 there were 26 British and Dutch boats based on Ceylon, and in the last six months of 1944 they sank 16 merchantmen totalling 35,562 tonnes (35,000 tons), together with two German U-boats and a Japanese submarine. Their main operating areas were the Malacca Straits, off Java and in the South China Sea. Many of their actions were against small craft, which they sank with gunfire; Japanese anti-submarine tactics werre inefficient and their small sub-chasers could sometimes be despatched in this way. Large targets were rare, and warship targets even more so; it was a noteworthy achievement when Cdr A.R. Hezlet in *Trenchant* sank the Japanese heavy cruiser *Ashigara* on 8 June 1945 as the warship was heading for Singapore, laden with troops from Batavia. Hezlet fired a salvo of eight torpedoes at long range and five of them hit their target.

Three British and four Dutch submarines were lost on operations in the Far East. Their claim was two cruisers, two destroyers, five U-boats, 13 minor naval vessels, 47 sizeable merchant ships and many small merchant craft. Seven of these ships are known to have been sunk by some of the 640 mines laid by submarines in the course of 30 operations. The sinkings added up, in total, to some 132,086 tonnes (130,000 tons) by the end of the war.

CHAPTER 7

LIMITED WARS: KOREA AND SUEZ

World War II was barely over when the Royal Navy found itself facing a series of new and smaller conflicts. The first major test was in Korea, 1950–53, and it was there that the Royal Navy's fleet carriers came into their own.

On 25 June 1950, North Korean forces, with Russian and Chinese backing, launched a massive invasion of the Republic of Korea. While United Nations forces strove to plug the widening gaps in South Korea's defences, a naval blockade of the Korean coast was rapidly established. On 30

ABOVE: Westland Whirlwind helicopters preparing to lift Royal Marine Commandos into action at Suez, November 1956, from the carrier Theseus. This was the first ever helicopter assault from the sea.

LEFT: The aircraft carrier HMS Eagle at speed, carrying Blackburn Buccaneers, Supermarine Scimitars and de Havilland Sea Vixens.

June, with the British Government's backing for United Nations action in Korea secured, the aircraft carrier HMS *Triumph* arrived in Korean waters from Hong Kong, accompanied by two cruisers, two destroyers and three frigates; on the following day, the USS *Valley Forge* and her escorts also took up station in the Yellow Sea, the Allied force operating under the designation of Task Force 77.

It was the British force that opened the naval war off Korea when, at dawn on 2 July 1950, the cruiser HMS *Jamaica* and the sloop *Black Swan* engaged six North Korean MTBs that were presenting a threat to the aircraft carriers, and sank five of them. At 0545 the next morning, the carrier aircraft flew their first strikes against targets in North Korea. Twelve

HMS TRIUMPH AND HER SISTERS – THE LIGHT BRIGADE

HMS *Triumph* was one of 17 light aircraft carriers commissioned in 1945–46. She served in the Far East and off Korea, and was converted to the role of heavy repair ship at Hong Kong in 1958–64. She was a member of the 13,400-tonne (13,190-ton) 'Colossus' class of small, unarmoured carriers which were a wartime expedient, being quick and simple to build. Destroyer machinery was fitted and they were equipped with a single hangar which could accommodate 48 aircraft. Of the ships in this class, *Colossus* served with the Pacific Fleet in 1945, and in 1946 she was loaned to France and named *Arromanches*; *Glory* also joined the Pacific Fleet in 1945, subsequently serving in the Mediterranean and in Korean waters, being broken up in 1961; *Ocean* served in the Mediterranean, Far East and off Korea and Suez, being broken up in 1962; *Theseus* had a similar career; *Venerable* was transferred to the Netherlands as the *Karel Doorman* in 1948; *Vengeance* was loaned to Australia in 1952 and was later sold to Brazil as the *Minas Gerais*; and *Warrior*, after service as HQ ship in the Christmas Island nuclear tests, was sold to Argentina as the *Independencia* in 1958. Two other vessels, *Edgar* and *Mars*, were completed as aircraft maintenance ships.

None of the 15,952-tonne (15,700-ton) 'Majestic' class of light carrier (*Hercules*, *Leviathan*, *Magnificent*, *Majestic*, *Powerful* and *Terrible*) saw service with the Royal Navy. All but *Leviathan* were completed for foreign navies, *Leviathan* being broken up incomplete in 1968.

Of the 18,594-tonne (18,300-ton) 'Hermes' class, *Albion* was converted to the commando carrier role in 1961–62 and was broken up in 1973; *Arrogant* was cancelled in 1945; *Bulwark* was converted as a commando carrier in 1959–60 and was decommissioned in 1981; *Centaur* operated an air group of Sea Vixens and Scimitars, serving mainly east of Suez, and was broken up in 1972; *Hermes* (originally named HMS *Elephant*) was converted to the commando role in 1971–73 and then as an ASW carrier in 1976, later (1982) serving as the Falklands Task Force flagship with an air group of Sea Harriers and Sea King helicopters before being sold to the Indian Navy as the *Virat* in 1986; and *Monmouth* and *Polyphemus* were cancelled in 1945.

Fairey Firefly fighter-bombers of No 827 Squadron and nine rocket-armed Seafire 47s of No 800 Squadron were launched by HMS *Triumph* to attack Haeju airfield, with railways and bridges as secondary targets. The aircraft all returned safely, although some had minor flak damage. The carriers mounted

further air strikes that day and on 4 July, destroying three hangars and some aircraft on the ground at Pyongyang, as well as bombing and strafing rolling stock and vehicles. The carriers withdrew from the combat zone for replenishment at sea on 5 July.

CLOSE SUPPORT

Air reconnaissance had revealed that the majority of the North Korean Air Force's serviceable aircraft were concentrated on the airfields of Pyongyang, Onjong-ni and Yonpo, and on 18 and 19 July these targets were heavily attacked by aircraft of Task Force 77 (USS *Valley Forge* and HMS *Triumph*), which claimed the destruction of 32 enemy aircraft on the ground and a further 13 damaged. The naval aircraft also hit railroads and factories. During the remainder of the month, Task Force 77 struck deep behind enemy lines and flew close-support missions as required, the carriers moving around the peninsula from the Sea of Japan to the Yellow Sea.

The naval close-support missions in these early stages were not particularly successful for a variety of reasons, not least being the fact that Air Force and Navy were using two different types of map. Naval pilots also found difficulty in establishing contact with the airborne controllers, known as 'Mosquitoes', so that in many cases they were reduced to flying around seeking targets of opportunity, with no guidance from anyone. The British element of Task Force 77, meanwhile, was experiencing growing problems with the serviceability and suitability of its aircraft, particularly the Seafires, which had a very restricted endurance and were prone to deck landing accidents because of their narrow-track undercarriage. In the end they were assigned to CAP duties over the fleet, leaving the American aircraft to concentrate on ground attack operations.

On 8 October 1950, additional striking power was added to Task Force 77 – which now comprised the US carriers *Boxer*, *Leyte*, *Philippine Sea*, and *Valley Forge* – in the shape of HMS *Theseus*, which relieved HMS *Triumph* in Korean waters. She had been in port in the UK when she was alerted for Korean duty in late August; the two squadrons of her 17th Carrier Air Group, No 807 with Hawker Sea Furies and No 810 with Fairey Fireflies, immediately embarked on a period of intensive training that lasted six weeks, both in the UK and while the carrier was en route to the Far East. *Theseus* went on active duty in the Yellow Sea on 9 October, launching her first sorties that same day. With its armament of four 20mm (0.8in) cannon and provision for up to 906kg (2000lb) of external stores, the Sea Fury was to provide a useful asset to Allied naval air power in Korea for the duration of hostilities.

HMS *Theseus* withdrew to Iwakuni for replenishment on 22 October, her Sea Furies and Fireflies having completed 264 and 120 sorties respectively. She returned to her war station early in November to cover minesweeping operations in the

ABOVE: The 'Colossus' class light carrier HMS Triumph entering Grand Harbour, Malta, in February 1947. Triumph was converted to the role of heavy repair ship in 1964.

Chinnampo estuary, then went to Hong Kong to take part in an exercise, having temporarily disembarked six of her Fireflies to carry out bombardment spotting duties.

After returning from the exercise at Hong Kong, *Theseus* mounted a series of strikes between 6 and 26 December 1950, the aircraft concentrating on roads, bridges, airfields and rolling stock. During this period CAG 17 flew 630 sorties, and anti-submarine patrols were flown by a Firefly fitted with a 250-litre (55-gallon) long-range tank in place of its radar. It was reported that the small North Korean Navy had two Russian-built submarines, believed to be active in the Yellow Sea, but they were not sighted. A combat air patrol was also maintained during daylight hours and a staggering total of 3900 interceptions and visual identifications was logged by the Sea Furies. All the aircraft intercepted proved to be Allied types, mainly B-29s, Neptunes and Sunderlands.

Top cover – up to 12,192m (40,000 feet) – for all strikes launched by *Theseus* and subsequent Commonwealth carriers operating off Korea was provided by the US Fifth Air Force, the strikes being directed by T-6 or L-4 'Mosquito' aircraft. Armed reconnaissance was the task of No 810 Squadron's Fireflies, flying at 456m (1500ft) or less over enemy territory – an increasingly risky business because of intense small arms fire. The information they and other UN reconnaissance aircraft brought back was coordinated by the Joint Operations Centre at Taegu, where one Royal Navy and two US Navy liaison officers analysed potential targets for assignment to the carrier aircraft. The high quality of the reconnaissance, resulting in very accurate and damaging air strikes, soon made enemy movements in daylight extremely hazardous. Bridges were among the main objectives. Following the early strikes, however, reconnaissance showed that the enemy was rebuilding these almost as quickly as the Fleet Air Arm

knocked them down, so from then on delayed action bombs were used to make this task more difficult. Because of the shallow waters off the Korean coast, *Theseus* had to stand off at a distance of up to 130km (70nm), a long haul for an aircraft suffering from battle damage. It was here that the 'plane guard' S-51 helicopters proved their worth; they rescued four ditched pilots and snatched four more from behind enemy lines.

In January and February 1951, aircraft from the *Theseus* were engaged in spotting for Allied naval forces bombarding Inchon. Afterwards, the carrier moved from her station on the west coast into the Sea of Japan, where between 9 and 19 April, in company with the US carrier *Bataan*, her aircraft spotted for warships shelling Wonsan and Songjin. It was the British carrier's final operation in Korean waters, where she had spent a total of six and a half months. During that time, her aircraft had made 3489 operational sorties, dropping 92

BELOW: Hawker Sea Furies of No 804 Squadron on HMS Glory wait to launch strikes against targets in Western Korea, 1952. These were the only piston-engined fighters to shoot down MiG-15s.

453kg (1000lb) and 1474 227kg (500lb) bombs, launching 7317 rocket projectiles and firing over half a million rounds of 20mm (0.8in) ammunition. Her pilots had never encountered any enemy aircraft. Many of the operational sorties had been flown in bad weather, particularly in December and January, when snowstorms often swept across the country without warning. *Theseus* was relieved by another light fleet carrier, HMS *Glory*, whose operations followed the pattern laid down by her predecessor. Throughout her tour, *Theseus* was supplied by the support carrier HMS *Unicorn*, bringing up spares and replacements from Singapore.

ABOVE: Arming a Hawker Sea Hawk jet fighter-bomber aboard HMS Eagle for a strike on Egyptian airfelds, November 1956. Sea Venoms and Wyverns also took part in the attacks.

On 31 May 1951, the UN Command implemented Operation Strangle, the object of which was to cut off the Main Line of Resistance (MLR) from the rest of North Korea by means of a concerted air offensive against the enemy's lines of communication, in a strip of territory stretching across Korea for a depth of one degree of latitude above 38°15'N. The road system was split up into eight main routes and all bridges, embankments, choke points, defiles and tunnels were placed on the target list. The three westernmost routes were assigned to the Fifth Air Force; the 1st Marine Air Wing was allocated the three easternmost; while Task Force 77 was given the two centre routes. Naval air strikes in the vicinity of the MLR, within the framework of Operation Strangle, were carried out by the Marine Air Wing and Task Force 95, the UN Blockading and Escort Force established in September 1950. Task Force 95 was split into two main elements, Task Group 95.1 – under British command and including most of the Commonwealth naval units – patrolling the west coast, and Task Group 95.2, patrolling the east coast from the MLR to the island of Yang-do. Operating with TG 95.1, the Sea Furies and Fireflies of HMS *Glory*'s 804 and 812 Squadrons were extremely active during Strangle. On one occasion in June, the British carrier

LEFT: HMS Ocean with a French hospital ship in the background, during Operation Musketeer, the Anglo-French attempt to seize control of the Suez Canal in 1956.

flew off 84 sorties in a single day, setting up a record that was only broken in October by the Australian carrier HMAS *Sydney*.

SEA FURY V MIG-15

Glory normally worked in a nine-day operation cycle, flying for four days in which she averaged a 14-hour flying day, replenishing for one day, returning for a second four-day period and then handing over to the US carrier *Bataan*, before going to Kure or Sasebo in Japan for maintenance and then returning for another nine-day cycle. By 22 June, her air group (CAG 14) had expended some 60,000 rounds of 20mm (0.8in) ammunition, over 1000 rockets and 180 bombs. During her tour, which ended on 21 September, she lost two Sea Furies and two Fireflies to enemy action, but all the aircrew with the exception of one Firefly pilot were picked up. As mentioned earlier, *Glory*'s relief, HMAS *Sydney* – with the Sea Furies of 805 and 808 Squadrons and the Fireflies of 817 embarked – broke the light carrier record with 89 sorties on 11 October 1951. But when *Glory* returned for a second tour in January 1952, after a refit in Australia, she put the record up to 104 sorties.

The summer of 1952 was notable for several deep-penetration missions by the enemy, the MiGs using their superior numbers to slip past the Sabre barrier and rove as far south as Haeju in search of Allied fighter-bombers. During one such mission, on 9 August, eight of them encountered the Sea Furies and Fireflies of HMS *Ocean*'s 802 and 825 Squadrons. *Ocean* was the only carrier to experience serious air opposition off the west coast. Already, on 27 July, four of 825 Squadron's Fireflies had been attacked by a pair of MiGs and two damaged, and soon afterwards four Sea Furies were attacked by four MiGs which caused no damage. The encounter of 9 August, however, turned into a full-blown air battle. It was described by Lieutenant Peter Carmichael, the flight leader, who recorded: 'The encounter that my flight had with the MiGs took place at 0600 hours. My No 2, Sub-Lt Carl Haines, said 'MiGs five o'clock'. I did not see them at first and my No 4, Sub-Lt 'Smoo' Ellis, gave a break. We all turned towards the MiGs. Two went for my Nos 3 and 4, Lt Pete Davies and Sub-Lt Ellis. They were seen to get good hits on one, who broke away with smoke coming from him.'

Carmichael also got in a good burst at a MiG, which went down and crashed. His report continues: 'Though I have been credited with shooting down the (Royal Navy's) first MiG, I feel that it was more of a flight effort than an individual one, because the one that crashed behind me was fired at by all of my flight. My Nos 3 and 4 then had another attack on them and got hits on this one. He broke away and the rest of the MiGs broke off the engagement and escorted him away. The impression we got was that these MiG pilots were very inexperienced and did not use their aircraft to any advantage at all. I think it was the next day that we had another engagement with eight MiGs and we were very lucky to get away

ABOVE: Precision attack on the airfield at Dekhelia by Westland Wyvern fighter-bombers of HMS Eagle's air group. The Wyvern was the first operational turboprop-powered combat aircraft.

with it. I reckon they must have sent the instructors down. These pilots put their aircraft to the best use and we managed to ease our way to some cloud that was about 20 miles away. One MiG got on my tail and my No 3 fired at him and he broke away. The only MiG who made a mistake was one who made a head-on attack on my Nos 3 and 4 and was hit by them and seen to go away with a lot of smoke and flame coming from him.'

During these two skirmishes, the pilots of 802 Squadron claimed the destruction of two MiG-15s, with three more damaged. To Lieutenant Carmichael fell the honour of becoming the first piston-engined pilot to shoot down an enemy jet in the Korean War. It was a formidable testimony to the Sea Fury's ruggedness and its excellent dogfighting characteristics.

The British aircraft carriers, and HMAS *Sydney*, operated in relays in Korean waters up to the armistice of June 1953. Although the contribution they made was relatively small compared with that of their larger and more numerous American counterparts, it was nevertheless significant; and it was to provide valuable operational experience when, three years later, the British carriers became involved in another 'limited' conflict.

SUEZ

In the summer of 1956, President Nasser of Egypt nationalised the Anglo-French Suez Canal Company and seized British and French assets in the Canal Zone. As a 'precautionary measure', a preliminary to possible armed intervention, units of the French Fleet were assembled at Toulon and three British aircraft carriers – HMS *Bulwark*, HMS *Theseus* and

HMS *Ocean* – were despatched to join HMS *Eagle* in the Mediterranean.

NAVAL STRIKES

There was also a critical shortage of vessels suitable for use as troopships. The first ships to be pressed into service in this role were the aircraft carriers *Ocean* and *Theseus*, which sailed for the Mediterranean at the end of July. Both vessels had been serving for some time as training ships and were no longer equipped to operate aircraft. A third carrier in British home waters, HMS *Bulwark*, had also been used for training, with her operational squadrons at shore bases. After embarking three squadrons of Hawker Sea Hawk Mk 6s she also sailed for the Mediterranean, arriving at Gibraltar on 9 August. Three days later she joined HMS *Eagle* off Malta and began an intensive period of flying training, her crews carrying out close-support operations in conjunction with No 45 Commando, air-to-air firing, practice shipping strikes on the frigate HMS *Ulysses* and the French carrier *Arromanches*, and low-level photo-reconnaissance.

While these exercises were still in progress the carrier HMS *Albion* also sailed for the Mediterranean following a refit; she arrived at the end of August and began working up her squadrons of Sea Hawks and Sea Venoms. En route to Malta she passed *Ocean* and *Theseus*, homeward bound once more after their initial period as troopships. On their return to the UK, both carriers were provided with more permanent accommodation for further troopship duties – *Ocean* was fitted with an operating theatre and extensive hospital facilities, which would enable her to be used as a hospital ship on station off the Egyptian coast during the operation.

A NEW ROLE

This re-equipment had hardly been completed when both ships were suddenly assigned a new role as helicopter carriers. HMS *Ocean* was to embark the Whirlwinds of No 845 Squadron, while *Theseus* was to take on the mixed complement of Sycamores and Whirlwinds belonging to the Joint Experimental Helicopter Unit (JEHU), a combined Army and RAF venture. This meant that many of the bunks newly erected in the carriers' hangars had to be taken out again. On 30 September, both carriers put to sea to practice helicopter operation techniques. Fourteen days later, No 845 Squadron was transferred from *Ocean* to *Theseus* in place of the JEHU aircraft, and the carrier sailed for Malta. Five days afterwards, *Ocean* also sailed for the Mediterranean after embarking JEHU.

At first light on 1 November, the land-based and carrier-borne strike squadrons took over the task of eliminating the Egyptian Air Force. Targets to the west of the 32° line of longitude were attacked by the Royal Navy's fighter-bombers, while those to the east were hit by the RAF ground attack aircraft from Cyprus. Thunderstreaks of the French Air Force were assigned to the role of providing top cover.

An hour before daybreak, as the last of the night's high-level bombers were returning to their bases, the Venom FB.4s of Nos 6, 8 and 249 Squadrons, together with the F-84Fs of the 3ème Escadre, took off from Cyprus on their first mission of the day. At the same time, 80km (50 miles) off the Egyptian coast, the aircraft carriers *Albion*, *Bulwark* and *Eagle* had turned into the wind and were preparing to launch their aircraft, having held their Wyverns, Sea Hawks and Sea Venoms at readiness for some hours. The two French light carriers, the *Arromanches* and *Lafayette*, with their complements of piston-engined Corsairs and Skyraiders, would cover the air and seaborne landings later on, once the Egyptian Air Force had been destroyed. In the meantime, their task was to seek out and disable Egyptian warships that might pose a threat to the inbound convoys.

The first naval strikes of the day were carried out by 40 aircraft from the three British carriers, which launched their squadrons at 0330 GMT to attack Cairo West, Almaza and Inchas. One high-priority target was assigned to a strike of Sea Hawks. This was an Egyptian tank landing ship, the *Akka*, which had been located in Lake Timsah. Indications were that it was about to be used to block the Canal. The attack was duly made and the pilots left the area under the impression that their target was sinking. In fact it was not, and the ship was towed into the Canal and sunk across the fairway, which remained blocked for several months.

AIRFIELD ATTACKS

The airfield attacks by the naval aircraft, meanwhile, had gone well. At Cairo West, Sea Hawk pilots from *Bulwark* found some Il-28s and left them in flames. Only light anti-aircraft fire was encountered, and all the aircraft returned safely to their carriers. Later in the day, when the carriers had established a steady rhythm, turning into wind and flying off strikes every few minutes, attacks were extended to the airfields at Bilbeis, Helwan and Heliopolis and to the coastal airfield of Dekhelia, near Alexandria, which was dive-bombed by Westland Wyverns from HMS *Eagle*. Another high-priority target, the Gamil Bridge – which carried the only road connecting Port Said to the Nile Delta – was assigned to the Royal Navy. It was dive-bombed by Sea Hawks and Wyverns of HMS *Eagle*'s air group, but it was a concrete structure with 11 supporting columns, and their bombs only succeeded in chipping large chunks off the columns. During this attack, a Wyvern flown by Lieutenant D.F. MacCarthy was hit by anti-aircraft fire; he limped out to sea, his aircraft smoking badly, and ejected. Although he had come down only 3658m (4000yds) from a shore battery, aircraft from *Eagle* and *Bulwark* maintained a defensive CAP overhead until a rescue helicopter arrived from *Eagle*, some 113km (70 miles) away. He was returned on board after two hours, unhurt.

In a second attack on the bridge, the Navy pilots changed their tactics, the Sea Hawks attacking at low level armed with 225kg (500lb) bombs with 30-second delay fuses.

ABOVE: A Supermarine Scimitar jet fighter-bomber, arrester hook extended, over the round-down of HMS Ark Royal. Originally named Irresistible, she served from 1950–79.

These penetrated the bridge and its supports like darts; the destructive effect of the explosions was enhanced by the confined spaces in which the bombs had lodged, and the bridge collapsed.

HMS *Albion* withdrew to refuel on 3 November in readiness to support the impending sea and airborne landings, but the other two carriers kept up a steady cycle of attacks. Egyptian forces, many of them withdrawn from Sinai, were flooding into the Cairo area, and the weight of the Allied fighter-bomber offensive continued to be directed against lines of communication. The roads running from the west towards Port Said soon became blocked with burnt-out transport and armoured fighting vehicles. The task of the fighter-bomber pilots was now complicated in that the roads were choked with refugees, streaming away from the Canal Zone, and great care had to be exercised to avoid attacking civilians by mistake.

Pilots returning from air strikes reported that the accuracy of the enemy anti-aircraft fire had now improved considerably, no doubt as the Egyptian gunners got used to coping with aircraft speeds of 640km/h (400mph) or more over the target. Since this growing efficiency posed a serious threat to the slow-flying transport aircraft which were to carry out the airdrop on the following Monday (it was now

Saturday), the strike aircraft were detailed to silence as many anti-aircraft batteries as possible, especially around Port Said. It was a difficult and dangerous task, and many of the aircraft returned to their carriers or airfields with varying degrees of battle damage.

On Sunday 4 November, with the invasion fleet approaching Egypt, HMS *Eagle* withdrew for replenishment and to receive replacement aircraft from El Adem. *Eagle's* crew made use of the break to repair the carrier's starboard catapult, which had been out of action during the whole operation. She returned to station that night, fully serviceable. HMS *Albion* was also back on station by now, so that the support carrier force was up to full strength.

Shortly before nightfall, Sea Hawks from HMS *Bulwark* made a successful attack with rockets and cannon on four Egyptian motor torpedo boats which had been reported by air reconnaissance to be heading out of Alexandria in the direction of the Naval Task Force. One boat blew up, two more were set on fire and the fourth was damaged but still able to pick up survivors.

On 6 November, following an airborne assault by British paratroops on Gamil airfield, waves of helicopters carrying men of No 45 Commando took off from the carriers *Ocean* and *Theseus* and headed for Port Said. It was the first helicopter assault in history, and a fitting climax to an operation which had proved yet again that the aircraft carrier was a vital component in projecting naval power across the world.

CHAPTER 8

THE COLD WAR ERA

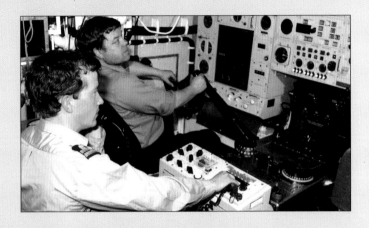

The dangerous years of the Cold War produced a new set of problems for the Royal Navy, not the least of which was the deployment of nuclear weapons and ballistic missile submarines. Anti-submarine warfare became of paramount importance for the survival of millions.

In the immediate post-war years, the great battleships and battlecruisers that had fought their way from the Arctic to the Pacific were early casualties of defence economy. By 1951, with one exception, all had been decommissioned, laid in reserve or broken up.

The exception was HMS *Vanguard*, an enlarged 'King George V' type battleship of 45,215 tonnes (44,500 tons).

ABOVE: The control room of the British nuclear submarine HMS Resolution. Depth, course and attitude are controlled by the helmsman, with the Officer of the Watch behind him.

LEFT: The Type 42 destroyer HMS Liverpool. The Type 42s were designed as small fleet escorts capable of area defence, and are armed with the Sea Dart surface-to-air missile system.

Launched in 1944, she was commissioned too late to see service in World War II. She was armed with eight 38cm (15in), 16 13cm (5.25in) and 71 40mm (1.6in) guns, and she carried a complement of 1600. Her four twin turrets mounted guns originally used in the *Courageous* and *Glorious* before their conversion to aircraft carriers. In 1947 she made a Royal Tour to South Africa and in 1949 served briefly in the Mediterranean before being placed on the reserve in 1956. She was decommissioned and sent to the breaker's yard at Faslane in 1960, the last battleship to serve in the Royal Navy.

The Royal Navy's new breed of capital ship at the end of World War II was the aircraft carrier; no fewer than 52 were in commission, ranging from the big fleet carriers of the 'Illustrious' and 'Implacable' classes to the small escort carriers that were converted merchantmen. The latter were soon

ABOVE: The Type 42 destroyer HMS Manchester *launching a Sea Dart SAM. The Sea Dart has proved to be very effective, and was used in the Falaklands in 1982 and in the Gulf War of 1991.*

withdrawn from use, many to revert to their peacetime commercial role, and of the fleet carriers only HMS *Victorious* survived beyond the mid-1950s, having undergone a major refit and modernization programme from 1950 to 1957.

In the late 1940s and early 1950s, it was the Royal Navy's Light Carriers that held the line. Some of their exploits are described in the previous chapter. Two new fleet carriers were building: the *Ark Royal*, laid down in 1943 and originally named *Irresistible*, and the *Eagle*, laid down in 1942 and originally named *Audacious*. Both were of 37,390 tonnes (36,800 tons) and were designed to carry 100 aircraft, although with the advent of heavier and more complex jet equipment this was later reduced to 36. *Eagle* was completed in 1951 and *Ark Royal* in 1955. Both underwent substantial reconstruction in the 1960s. A new class of carrier, the CVA-01, which was to have replaced them, was cancelled.

Soviet expansion worldwide in the 1950s led to a requirement for a naval intervention force capable of rapid

deployment. Two of the light carriers, *Albion* and *Bulwark*, were converted as commando carriers in the early 1960s, and two assault ships, *Fearless* and *Intrepid*, were completed in 1965 and 1967 respectively, these vessels together forming the main equipment of the Royal Navy's Amphibious Warfare Squadron.

NEW DESTROYERS

The 1950s saw the emergence of a new class of destroyer, the 'Daring' class, which were designed to fulfil several roles, including cruiser reconnaissance, anti-ship or anti-submarine patrols. At 2844 tonnes (2800 tons) they were the largest destroyers built for the Royal Navy up to that time. Other destroyers, of the 'Battle' class – HMS *Agincourt*, for example –were converted to the role of fleet radar pickets, while the 'County' class destroyers of the early 1960s were fitted out with a guided missile armament.

The first real test of the Royal Navy's 'rapid response' capability came in July 1958, when the threat of war once again loomed in the Middle East. The Lebanon was torn by internal strife and her territory was being infiltrated by Syrian troops. On 15 July, the pro-Western government of

Iraq was overthrown by a military coup and the Iraqi royal family massacred. Both King Hussein of Jordan and President Chamoun of the Lebanon asked Britain and the United States to intervene, fearing that their own governments would topple in turn.

On 16 July, US Marines went ashore in the Lebanon and on the following day the first elements of the British 16th Parachute Brigade, the veterans of Suez, arrived in the Jordanian capital of Amman. Meanwhile, units of the Royal Navy were being assembled to counter any emergency, including possible Soviet intervention. The fleet carrier HMS *Eagle* sailed from Malta and took up station to the east of Cyprus, accompanied by the cruiser *Sheffield* and a screen of destroyers and frigates, and her Sea Hawk and Sea Venom aircraft maintained regular patrols within sight of the Lebanese coast. The carrier HMS *Albion* arrived soon afterwards, having ferried No 42 Royal Marine Commando

from Portsmouth to Malta. HMS *Bulwark*, in the meantime, had sailed from Mombassa to Aden with the 1st Battalion, the King's Own Regiment. At Aden, she embarked the 1st Battalion of the Cameronians and ferried them up the Red Sea to the Jordanian port of Aqaba.

The rapid deployment of troops by the Royal Navy, the US Sixth Fleet and the RAF had the desired effect. By the beginning of November, the tension had eased sufficiently to permit the withdrawal of most units. The Royal Navy's first major exercise in the rapid movement of troops to counter the threat of a possible conflict had worked well, and set the pattern for future operations of this kind that Britain would take part in.

*BELOW: **The Amphibious Transport Dock (LPD) vessel HMS** Fearless, **together with HMS** Intrepid, **provided amphibious assault lift capability, using an onboard naval assault group.***

CONFRONTATION

Three years later, in July 1961, the Royal Navy played a leading part in preventing yet another Middle East crisis when the sheikhdom of Kuwait was threatened by an Iraqi invasion. HMS *Bulwark* was quickly on the scene, her Westland Whirlwind helicopters ferrying Royal Marine Commandos into Kuwait, and the carriers *Centaur* and *Victorious* were also sent to the region, both armed with de Havilland Sea Vixen jet fighter-bombers. Royal Navy warships – notably the commando carriers *Bulwark* and *Albion* – were also active during the confrontation between Malaysia and Indonesia in the early 1960s, and between 1964 and the end of 1967, Buccaneers, Sea Vixens and Scimitars from the Royal Navy's fleet carriers were active over troubled Southern Arabia, carrying out surveillance and the occasional strike against dissident tribes in the Radfan area.

In November 1967, following the British government's decision to bring forward the date of Southern Arabia's independence, the Royal Navy assembled the biggest task force since the Suez operation of 1956 in the Gulf of Aden to cover the British withdrawal. The task force was split into two groups. The first consisted of the commando carrier *Bulwark*, the assault ship *Fearless* and the fleet carrier *Eagle*, whose squadrons were responsible for providing air cover. The second group, consisting of HMS *Albion*, the assault ship *Intrepid* and the carrier *Hermes*, took up station later in the month. The final stages of the withdrawal were covered by the Royal Marines, and the Wessex helicopters of 845 and 848 Squadrons were the last naval aircraft to leave the area.

Meanwhile, a major revolution had taken place in the operational capability of the Royal Navy. At the end of World War II, the most advanced class of submarine

LEFT: The Royal Navy's Type 23 'Duke' class frigates are highly manoeuvrable, as this photograph shows. Sixteen have been commissioned. The ship in the picture is HMS Monmouth (F235).

The ballistic missile submarines (SSBNs) were followed by successive classes of nuclear attack submarines (SSNs). First came the 'Valiant' class of the late 1960s (*Valiant* and *Warspite*), which were essentially enlarged Dreadnoughts; they were followed by the 'Churchill' class (*Churchill*, *Conqueror* and *Courageous*); the 'Swiftsure' class (*Swiftsure*, *Sovereign*, *Superb*, *Sceptre*, *Spartan* and *Splendid*); and 'Trafalgar' class (*Trafalgar*, *Turbulent*, *Tireless*, *Torbay*, *Trenchant*, *Talent* and *Triumph*).

DANGEROUS GAP

In parallel with this new undersea capability, British shipbuilders produced a new generation of surface warships. These included the Type 82 destroyer HMS *Bristol*, which was originally intended to have been the lead ship of a class of four vessels designed to provide anti-submarine warfare (ASW) and surface-to-air missile protection for the cancelled CVA-01 aircraft carriers; and the Type 42 class, comprising HMS *Sheffield*, *Birmingham*, *Cardiff*, *Coventry*, *Newcastle*, *Glasgow*, *Exeter*, *Southampton*, *Nottingham*, *Liverpool*, *Manchester*, *Gloucester*, *York* and *Edinburgh*.

The frigate was an important part of the Royal Navy's warship inventory during the years of the Cold War. The 'Leander' class of general purpose frigate, which entered service in the 1960s, served the Navy well for many years, 26 of which were built.

The Leanders were to have been succeeded by 26 examples of the Type 22 'Broadsword' class, conceived as ASW ships for use in the Greenland-Iceland-UK gap against Soviet high-performance nuclear submarines; in the event only 14 were produced. The other principal class of frigate was the Type 21 'Amazon' class, of which eight were constructed.

The cancellation of the projected CVA-01 aircraft carrier class left the Royal Navy with a dangerous maritime air power gap, for its existing aircraft carriers were all due to be decommissioned by the end of the 1970s. In the late 1960s the Naval Staff began studies of a new class of ship, much smaller than CVA-01 (which was to have displaced 50,800 tonnes/50,000 tons) and without catapults or arrester wires. The new ship was intended for rotary-wing operations in northern waters; the fact that she would also be capable of operating short take-off/vertical landing (STOVL) aircraft like the British Aerospace Harrier, then flying in prototype form, was played down at the time.

The design was committed to manufacture in 1972 as HMS *Invincible*, the first of a new class of ASW carrier. She was laid down in 1973 and launched in 1977; her sister ships, *Illustrious* and *Ark Royal*, were laid down in 1976 and 1978 respectively. Their normal air group was to comprise

building for the Royal Navy was the 'A' class, designed for extended operations in the Pacific. The 'A' boats came too late for war service, and of 45 planned, only 18 were completed. The first post-war patrol submarine design was the 'Porpoise' class, eight of which were launched between 1957 and 1959; these were followed by 13 'Oberon' class boats, completed between 1961 and 1964. It was a submarine bearing a famous name – HMS *Dreadnought* – that brought about the revolution. Launched in October 1960 and commissioned in April 1963, she was the Royal Navy's prototype nuclear-powered submarine. By the spring of 1968, four nuclear-powered ballistic missile submarines – *Renown*, *Repulse*, *Resolution* and *Revenge* – had been launched; armed with 16 American Polaris missiles each, they took over the British nuclear deterrent role from the RAF in the late 1960s and continue to do so today.

ABOVE: *The Type 22 (Batch 2) frigate HMS Beaver (F93) with a Westland Lynx helicopter. The Batch 2s suffered heavily in the Falklands War, which led to an improved Batch 3 design.*

eight Sea Harrier strike fighters and 11 Sea King ASW helicopters.

In the event, HMS *Invincible* and many of the other warships mentioned above were to see combat in a region far removed from the northern waters in which they would have confronted the might of the Soviet Navy in a devastating World War III.

EXOCET

On 2 April 1982 an Argentinian amphibious group occupied the Falkland Islands. Britain's response was to assemble a task force to retake the islands; at its core was the aircraft carrier HMS *Hermes*, which in the 1970s had been configured as a helicopter-only ASW vessel but which had now been fitted with a 'ski ramp' for the operation of 12 Sea Harriers. As task force flagship, she sailed from Plymouth on 5 April, together with the *Invincible*. Two days later, the 'County' class guided missile destroyer HMS *Antrim* and the 'Rothesay' class antisubmarine frigate HMS *Plymouth*, together with the Royal Fleet Auxiliary vessel *Tidespring*, were detached to recapture

the island of South Georgia, which had also been illegally occupied. The Type-22 frigate *Brilliant* was also ordered to reinforce the South Georgia group, and the Argentine garrison surrendered on 26 April after a bombardment by *Antrim* and *Plymouth*.

Subsequent operations off the Falklands revealed some serious British shortcomings, one of which was the lack of airborne early warning, which meant that warships had to be deployed as radar pickets. One of them, the Type-42 destroyer HMS *Sheffield*, was damaged and set on fire in an Exocet air-to-surface missile attack while operating in this role, and had to be abandoned.

The initial landings to recover the Falklands took place on the night of 20–21 May, and the seven warships covering the attack subsequently fought a bitter battle against Argentinian fighter-bombers. HMS *Antrim*, acting as air defence coordinator, was an early casualty, being hit by a bomb which failed to explode and further damaged by strafing attacks; her role was taken over by the frigate *Brilliant*. The 'Leander' class frigate *Argonaut* was hit in a Skyhawk attack, but the bombs again failed to detonate; HMS *Ardent* was less lucky, being hit by nine bombs, seven of which exploded. She had to be abandoned.

On 23 May a new arrival, the Type-21 frigate *Antelope*, was hit by a bomb which failed to explode, but which later went off during disposal operations, sinking her. Two days later, HMS *Coventry* was sunk and HMS *Broadsword* damaged while they were acting as a missile trap to the north of the islands; and on that same day, the transport *Atlantic Conveyor* was sunk in a further Exocet attack. The landing ship *Sir Galahad* was subsequently destroyed by air attack when about to disembark troops at Bluff Cove, with heavy loss of life.

Without the two supporting aircraft carriers and their Sea Harriers, together with RAF Harrier ground attack aircraft brought in as reinforcements, a British victory in the Falklands would have been impossible. Aircraft from the *Hermes* and *Invincible* accounted for 33 of the enemy, in the air and on the ground. But there was no escaping the fact that some of the British warships that fell victim to air attack might have been saved had it not been for peacetime economic pressures that robbed them of significant close-range air defence systems and incorporated cheap, highly flammable materials into their design.

After the Falklands War modifications came thick and fast. The Type-23 or 'Duke' class of frigate, for example, originally intended as a cheap one-for-one replacement for the Leanders and the very costly Type-22s, was radically altered in the light of lessons learned in the Falklands conflict; 13 were built from the mid-1980s, beginning with HMS *Norfolk*. And when Royal Navy warships were deployed to the Arabian Gulf for operations in 1991, they were armed not only with long-range Sea Dart and short-range Seawolf missiles – both of

which had performed well in the Falklands – but also with Phalanx, an American automatic system based on a six-barrelled Gatling gun that is computer controlled, highly accurate against both aircraft and sea-skimming missiles, and fires an incredible 3000 rounds per minute against incoming targets. Never again would the Royal Navy be caught out in such a brutal fashion as it was in the cold waters of the South Atlantic in 1982.

BELOW: HMS Resolution was the Royal Navy's first powered ballistic missile submarine (SSBN), and was armed with 16 Polaris A3TKs. Five boats in this class were commissioned, at least two being on station at any one time.

CHAPTER 9

INTO THE 21ST CENTURY

Far from being unwanted following the collapse of the end of the Cold War, the Royal Navy will face a new set of demanding tasks as it supports NATO and United Nations peacekeeping tasks. This will require new equipment and new tactics.

The Royal Navy of the early twenty-first century is likely to be a service of contrasts. At one end of the scale, the massive Trident submarines – successors to the Polaris boats – will continue to patrol the oceans, an insurance against any dictator who might try to hold Britain to ransom by

ABOVE: The Royal Navy's new helicopter carrier, HMS Ocean, was designed to replace the assault ships Fearless and Intrepid. Fully laden, her helicopters can airlift a battalion of 830 commandos.

LEFT: The 'Vanguard' class SSBN HMS Victorious setting out on her first patrol. Commissioned in January 1995, she is armed with 16 Trident 2D5 missiles with MIRV warheads.

threatening the use of weapons of mass destruction; at the other, Royal Navy warships will have an increasing role to play as peacekeepers within the NATO infrastructure, acting on behalf of the United Nations.

Many of the vessels that will serve the Royal Navy into the twenty-first century – the Tridents, for example (*Vanguard, Victorious, Vigilant* and *Vengeance*) – were born of Cold War requirements; three planned large nuclear-powered attack submarines of 6400 tonnes (6300 tons), evolved from the 'Trafalgar' class and named *Astute, Ambush* and *Artful*, also fall into this category, as does the new helicopter carrier HMS *Ocean*. Designed to replace the assault ships *Fearless* and *Intrepid*, both of which were placed in reserve, *Ocean* was

ABOVE: ***Completed in May 1974, the Type 21 frigate HMS** Amazon* *was the only one of her class not to see action in the Falklands War. Their aluminium superstructure proved to be a fire risk.*

commissioned in August 1998 and displaces 22,107 tonnes (21,758 tons) fully laden; her helicopters can airlift a battalion of 830 Royal Marine Commandos. Other new vessels, still in the project stage at the turn of the century, include the 'Horizon' class air-defence ship, planned jointly with Italy and France; the Royal Navy has a requirement for 12 of these vessels.

STEALTH SHIPS

Sea warfare will never be the same again. The titanic mid-ocean battles that were a scenario of the Cold War will never be enacted. Instead, future naval battles will be fought along coastlines against developing countries or small regional powers. The navy of the future will be optimised for shallow water warfare, and in this respect minehunting vessels will come into their own, for mines will present a serious risk to inshore operations. Britain's 'Hunt' class mine-countermeasures vessels, 13 of which are in service, are constructed from glass-reinforced plastic to give maximum protection.

'Stealthy' warships, capable of approaching a hostile coastline and operating undetected within sight of it, are already in an advanced stage of development. In 1997, British shipbuilders Vosper Thorneycroft unveiled a 'Stealth' ship called *Sea Wraith II*, which employs various deception devices. For example, it has a mast fitted with various dihedral and trihedral shapes which strongly reflect radar signals, masking the ship's true radar signature. In war conditions, the mast would be lowered, so that *Sea Wraith* would present an entirely different radar signature.

Sea Wraith is also camouflaged in the thermal part of the spectrum, to defend against heat-seeking missiles. A ship's thermal signature comes mainly from the engine exhaust, which heats up the funnels. To minimize this effect, *Sea Wraith* passes its exhaust fumes through sea water before expelling them, so that all that emerges from the funnels are cool gases.

Measures such as this, however, are not enough to confuse the latest generation of anti-ship missiles, which home in on

RIGHT: ***The aircraft carrier HMS** Invincible, **with Sea Harriers on deck. The Sea Harrier proved a decisive weapon in the Falklands, but lacked an adequate airborne early warning systems.***

ABOVE: The Type 82 class destroyer HMS Bristol was originally intended to have been the lead ship of a class of four vessels designed to protect the cancelled CVA-01 aircraft carriers.

BELOW: The Sea Wraith II is a futuristic 'Stealth' frigate design by the British firm Vosper Thorneycroft, which has great experience in the design of fast patrol and attack craft.

their target using thermal video images. They are almost impossible to distract with flares, which look nothing like ships to high resolution imagers. The only way to protect the ship is to hide it entirely – which is exactly what *Sea Wraith's* design team has done. *Sea Wraith* has a cloaking device that hides the whole ship from sensors in the visible and infrared regions. The vessel will be fitted with thousands of tiny nozzles that spray atomised water into the air, enveloping the ship in a giant cloud of fine water droplets. This absorbs both short- and long-wavelength infrared as well as visible light, but allows the ship's radar to function normally.

TRIMARANS

Another project that might one day form a vital component of the Royal Navy's sea power is the Stealth Trimaran Aircraft Carrier (STAC), which is being investigated as an option to replace the existing 'Invincible' class aircraft carriers. Designed by Avpro UK, STAC would be faster, longer, wider, more stable and far less vulnerable to attack than any existing British carrier. Incorporating the latest 'Stealth' technology, it would have a radar signature similar to that of a fishing trawler. Displacing some 40,000 tonnes (39,368 tons), it would carry 55 aircraft and have a maximum speed of 40 knots.

The trimaran hull configuration would permit STAC to have a flight deck 100m (328ft) wide, permitting up to 30

aircraft to be prepared for launch at any one time. The main central hull would be more than 300m (984ft) long, providing space for one long runway, plus a 'ski jump' ramp at the bow for STOVL aircraft, and two shorter runways running diagonally across an angled deck. Conventional aircraft would be catapulted from the flight deck using a very powerful electromagnetic rail system, and land with the aid of advanced arrester gear using special dampers. The two outrigger hulls would protect the central hull from torpedoes and missiles, and would keep the carrier afloat in the event of severe damage.

A vessel like STAC would cost about £3 billion per unit, which raises the question of whether the nation could afford it. Whether it could afford not to have it, and other such advanced warships, in a post-Cold War world that is likely to become even more dangerously unstable, is another matter.

ABOVE: HMS Ocean *forms the centrepiece of this depiction of the Royal Navy carrying out a helicopter assault. An 'Albion' class assault ship is on the right and Type 23 'Duke' class frigates provide air defence with vertical-launch Seawolf missiles.*

RIGHT: Depiction of a Type 23 'Duke' class frigate moving at speed, accompanied by a EH-101 Merlin HAS-1 helicopter. The Dukes are based with the 4th Frigate Squadron at Portsmouth and the 6th Frigate Squadron at Devonport.

INDEX